heal my
BR♥KEN
wing

HOW TO REBUILD
AFTER HEARTBREAK

Laverne Thomas

HEAL MY BROKEN WING

Author: Laverne Thomas

ISBN-13: 978-0692110652

ISBN-10: 0692110658

LCCN: TBD

Editing/Typesetting/Book Cover: Young Dreams Publications

Connect with Laverne Thomas

Email: laverne@blissdreamlove.org
Website: www.blissdreamlove.com
Facebook: Bliss Dream Love Consults
Twitter & IG: @blissdreamlove

Author Bio

Laverne Thomas is a mother of two beautiful children from Chicago. She hails from a large family, born number 5 in a family of 9 children, from loving and caring parents. She is a double Master's college graduate and has 15+ years serving families in the urban communities and academic institutions.

She is also the author of *Love on Fire*, her first book which debuted in 2015. *Love on Fire* is a book geared toward supplying guidance on how to rekindle the romance and communication within relationships. The book can be purchased at blisslovedream.com or on Amazon.

Hit like a strong wind in mid-flight!

"Oh Lord God, have mercy
on me, and heal my broken wing!"- Khalil Gibran

I have been known to be a cry baby in my life. I'm extremely sensitive so crying just comes with the program. I have a soft heart but I love hard. And typically the harder I love the more painful disappointments, lies, and deceits affect me. Although I've been through heart break before, this one was record breaking for me. The cry I gave out was unlike anything I had ever heard or experienced from myself. It was loud but silent, deep and painful, dark and tender, and foulest of all it was mine. It had an echo, too; a hard echo that consistently pierced my own hearing. This cry wouldn't stop. I never knew I had so many trapped tears screaming to be set free until then.

It made me feel faint. I could barely stand. The only thing I wanted to do was lie down not, even on my bed but underneath it, and never come out. I didn't want to see or hear from anyone. Nobody could fix this hurt. Nobody could

1

soothe this unexpected pain that had seized my entire body inside and out. Nothing could make it stop. It was unreal, unfair, and undeserving. This cry and pain was devastating. It was a cry caused by a man that I loved more than anything else in this world. A man who promised to love me, honor me, and cherish me forever. This cry was created out of selfishness, disrespect, ignorance, and unfaithfulness. It was something created for me and was something I never wanted. And now I had to figure out what in the world to do with it.

It made me face myself, my truths, and my life in a way I never had to do before. I had to learn everything all over from scratch. I had to pick up pieces of myself and my life that I didn't even know were broken. It forced me into a place that was dark, without the slightest glimpse of light. I had nowhere to go but through it in order to reach the other side of pain. This new life or journey was hard, rough, and raw. It peeled away at me mentally, emotionally, spiritually, and physically. It opened wounds, caused scars, and created scabs over past hurts. It took me through it. But it was something I couldn't avoid or escape. It was something I had to experience in order to get to reach the next level in my life.

What I experienced was new to me but not uncommon. Women feel that hurt every day, all over the world. Some deal with it well and some don't know what to do with it at all. It may seem extremely hard initially to see pass the pain. We can't see ourselves loving again, trusting again, or even living after someone has hurt us so badly. We need examples of where to go or what to do. We need someone to help guide us from the pain and into joy again. We need someone to help us see that this won't last always. We just need someone. That one friend you can trust or a confidant you can rely on. Someone who has moved passed the bitterness, self-doubt, self-pity, and pain and now is living life again. Someone who has been healed and made whole.

> *What I experienced was new to me but not uncommon.*

Sometimes that person is near, sometimes they are far and sometimes there is no one like that in sight. That's why I've written this book. I want to be the someone that helps you get through one of the roughest times in your life. I want to be your guide because I've been down a similar road and made it to the other side. God has given me a map that I followed and I want to share it with you. I want to wipe tears, give hugs, and speak life into those who don't see anything right now but darkness. I want to be that someone and the easiest way to do that is through sharing my story with you in hopes that it will help.

Since I was a teen I have experienced pain from men consistently that some would wonder how I am even standing now. How do I still believe in love? How can I remain so positive? After my most recent heartbreak, which was the failure of my marriage, I evaluated every relationship that I have been through. I was able to reflect on where things went wrong and what decisions I could

> Sometimes that person is near, sometimes they are far and sometimes there is no one like that in sight.

have made to put myself in better situations. That reflection gave me a perspective that I didn't have before and it ultimately helped me make it through the worst kind of pain I have ever experienced. These were lessons learned that I'm ultimately going to share with you through ten chapters. These chapters are pieces of my heart written in black and white just for you. These chapters are honest, genuine, and transparent. Transparency is an intentional approach because it is something that can be felt, understood, and respected. And I wanted to start our journey together the right way so you can trust that I'm leading you in the right direction - and that's toward healing.

Why would I do this? Because nothing speaks to a broken heart better than another broken heart. My transparency will reach those broken pieces of you, and help piece you back together again. It was done for me and now it's only right that I return the favor for you. It will be my complete honor to assist you through this journey. Let's go!

Chapter 1
This Pain Has Got to Go!

White Dove

Doves have symbolized the Holy Spirit, love, peace, hope, and the soul for centuries. As a result of this, many people release doves at funerals as a symbol of their loved ones no longer feeling pain. They are now in complete peace and free from hurt.

"He Heals the broken hearted and bandages their wounds"
Psalm 147:3 MSG

"That's why I don't think there is any comparison between the present hard times and the coming of good times."
Romans 8:18 MSG

It took me a great deal of time to get passed the pain I felt from the end of my marriage. This journey was a year and a half long. The clock started a day in November that we mutually agreed to separate. That day I felt the most pain and the most relief at the same time. Yes, our marriage was turbulent with more than a few hard times for us both. But the day we decided we no longer wanted to be with each other cut deep. This was the end of a ten-year friendship, bond, and love. A connection like that, rather good or bad, is hard to dissolve. But it did. And now I had to deal with it accordingly. And this is how I did it.

Feel it!

I am by far the most sensitive person ever. I cry at sad movies or tragic stories on the news. I cried when my previous spouse yelled at me or raised his voice. I cry when I remember painful situations that happened years ago. The point is I feel everything. Rather it has something to do with me directly or not. That's just the way I am and there is nothing wrong with that, despite being told otherwise. God made me with a soft heart and that's one of my greatest gifts. But it can also be my greatest weakness.

When I separated from my pervious spouse, I surprised myself. I tried not to feel anything. This was because I didn't want my children to see me hurting or falling apart. I wanted to be strong for them. So I bottled everything, good or bad, inside. I was pretty much operating as a robot. I was performing out of routine and schedules. Nothing was heartfelt or genuine. It was all things I had to do to function and nothing more. It sounds crazy when I think about it now, but it worked for me for a few months - until it didn't anymore. One day I got up like any typical morning. I got the kids ready for school, dropped them off and started on my way to work. And then it came tumbling down. On the expressway, alone in my car I couldn't hold it in anymore. I cried and cried and cried until I had to eventually pull over being afraid that I would crash.

Everything became so real at that very moment. See in this season I didn't just lose my husband, but my father passed away just a few months earlier. And he was my very best friend in the entire world. We had an amazing relationship. I was the ultimate daddy's girl. And losing him was devastating. But I couldn't grieve him because I was busy dealing with my marriage. But once the marriage was gone and I faced my own reality things began to feel horrible. So that day in my car I wasn't just crying over my marriage. It was the realization that I had lost my father and my husband at the same time. The two men who meant the world to me were suddenly no longer present in my life. And it felt unbearable. I thought nothing could feel worse than what I was feeling at that very moment in life. But that moment in life created a change in my life for the better. I just couldn't see it then. But I see it now.

What that moment taught me is that it's okay to feel. It's more than okay, it's essential in the healing process. I was stuck in my pain until I allowed myself to feel that day. And from that day on, each day I was able to come to terms with my new life. I was able to see my current situation for what it was and deal with it each day differently. Each day was new and came with different emotions. Every day I smiled in front of people around me rather at home or at work. This was my game face. I didn't want anyone to know how horrible I was feeling inside so they wouldn't start asking me questions. Because eventually I would have to answer those questions and speaking about it – which only made me cry even harder. So I wore my smile like makeup until I didn't have to anymore. But whenever I was alone, rather in the bathroom or in my car, I cried. Even if it was just

> *What that moment taught me is that it's okay to feel. It's more than okay, it's essential in the healing process.*

a single tear that fell or a whole rainforest of tears, I cried. And this happened every day until it didn't.

I can't tell you the specific day or time when it didn't hurt so bad anyone. But I can tell you one day it didn't hurt as much. One day I got up with energy and smiled a genuine smile. One that you can see through my eyes and can feel if you were near me. One day I didn't feel like a failure and that I could right every wrong in my life. That one day made all of those sad days seem like a distant memory. And every day from that day I tried harder and harder to get back to me. And getting back to me was being truly happy no matter what the situation I had to face.

When you are rebuilding, understand that the pain will come one day and it may go away the next. But when it reappears, it's okay to feel it and release it in a way that works. You have the right to cry, scream, throw things, write it out, or whatever else you need to do to get that pain out. Any method of release is good except those that put you or someone else in harm's way. So please seek professional help if you are feeling this way. But no one can tell you how to feel. No one knows the pain you are experiencing besides you. Feeling that pain makes you human. Ignoring it only makes it worse and stagnates your growth and healing. Never sweep your feelings and emotions under the rug.

Doing this is dangerous to your mental and emotional health. Eventually you will have a home full of lumpy rugs, making it hard to walk over. And no one wants a house they can't walk freely in.

Allowing yourself to feel the pain is hard. I know this to be a fact. Nothing I tell you is going to be anything I haven't personally experienced. The length of time getting through and over pain is unique to each person. You may be able to feel it and let it go in a short amount of time, but it may also take you a while. Either way it's alright. And never compare your process to your previous mates. Things are not always what they seem. Just because they are in a new relationship already and appear to be doing so well without you, don't let that hold you back. Don't allow that anger and frustration alter your journey. Walk your walk at your own pace. It's not a race and no one is timing you. The ultimate goal is not to win first place but simply just to finish.

> *It's not a race and no one is timing you.*

Whatever you do with your pain, don't stay there in it. At some point you have to want more for your life and you have to move on. Sometimes you may feel like you are over it and realize you are not. That's normal. That's because being hurt by someone you love is like a bruise. When the bruise first surfaces you can see it clearly. It's dark, comes in many shapes, and hurts like hell. But over time it will get better. But if you don't nurture that bruise correctly, it can stay longer than expected. And whenever you touch it, the tenderness is still there reminding you of that very thing (or person) that put it there in the first place. And that's how broken wings feel. If you don't take the proper steps to heal after a heartbreak, your heart becomes bruised. Every time you think of that person, hear a song, see their face on social media, or smell their cologne, it's like touching that tender spot every time. Even when you close your eyes, you can feel it even more. So please, allow yourself to feel the hurt and make your way through the pain.

Recognize it!

This right here took me a long time to realize. Besides sitting in my pain for too long, I truly believe this is what held me back the longest from getting healed. I was unable to recognize what I was really hurt by. What seemed obvious really wasn't and what it actually was, was beyond my understanding.

When you get hurt, one of the next things that you have to do is understand and recognize just what part of the event hurt you. I know you are probably thinking, "What is she talking about? My man hurt me. That's it!" Yes, he was the driver, but before the car hit you there were some circumstances that occurred that caused the crash. So essentially what I'm asking is what about the entire situation caused you the most pain? For instance, let's say you were involved in a car accident. Ultimately, it was the car that caused the collision. The car was the large force that caused the damage. But how did the car get there? Who was driving it? And what caused the driver to lose control of their vehicle and cause you pain? What or who was the real reason for your pain?

It wasn't my previous spouse's actions that specifically hurt me. It was everything that his actions represented. Here is what I mean. I was in a relationship with my previous spouse ten years. We dated for five and were married for five. From the moment we started dating I was in love with him. It was instant almost. He was pretty much everything I asked God for in my prayers. I wrote a letter to God one year and listed twenty-five things I wanted my future husband to be. These were different personality traits, personal goals, family values, etc. Things I thought were important and that made a great mate for me. So when I met my previous spouse, he matched everything on my list except one thing. And it meant so much to me because I wrote that list a few months before I met him and placed it in my Bible. So I knew for sure God sent him my way.

With me figuring this has got to be him and the fact that he was such a great person, our relationship moved quickly. Because I am passionate and I love hard, I became everything to and for him. No matter what it was, I did it. No matter what he needed, I provided it. No matter what was missing, I found it. I loved that man beyond understanding. I became the wife even before I had a ring! I was faithful, loyal, protective, and loving. I tried my best to meet every need that he had. And I did. I was the very example of the perfect woman. I never questioned his whereabouts, never considered he wasn't truthful, nor thought anything was ever wrong. It was perfect to me. I did everything with intentionality and expectation that he would see just how wonderful I was. And he did because ultimately he proposed to me and wanted me forever.

Sounds great, right? So what happened? Well, life happened. When I discover years later that my perfect man wasn't so perfect, I was devastated. The man I never had to worry about clearly had time to spend with other women. I created a perfect reality of him and our relationship that I couldn't see that coming at all. And no matter who she or they were, it wasn't their existence that hurt me. It wasn't another woman or disrespect itself that caused me so much pain. It was the fact that everything I based our love on, trust, honesty, loyalty and friendship, was all unraveled in one moment. My pain was caused by a false foundation that I built my life on. It felt as if years of my life were flushed down the drain and I felt blindsided. I felt like the man I admired for so many years became unrecognizable to me. I didn't know this man that I learned about. But there he was. And I was faced with the question, "Now what do I do with him?"

I had to recognize that it was not the act of anything he did that broke, not only, my heart but my soul, but it was what it took from me that did. It took my friend, my memories, and my love away. That's why I couldn't move on. That's why I was stuck for so long. No matter what he did, he didn't put back together what this pain broke in pieces. I was waiting, begging, and pleading with him to do something. Anything! I didn't know if I wanted him to make some grand gesture to make it all better or just simply leave me alone. I just needed him to do something and do it quickly because I was hurting. I wanted him to make me whole again or at least half way full.

He would always say he didn't know what he could do. And although that would cause me a great deal of anger every time he said it, ultimately he was right. If I couldn't recognize why I was hurting, how could he fix it? He was not a mind reader. He didn't know what to do. In his mind it was all physical and couldn't begin to understand that it was emotional, spiritual and mental for me. I couldn't even, at the time, explain to him what it was. I was so blinded by hurt that all I could see was those women. And because he didn't even try to fix it out of lack of knowledge, I was left with a broken heart that never got repaired. And although we tried for a few years after that, we never really got back on the right course.

So when I say, recognize the pain, you have to do just that. Not for the other person but for yourself. When you recognize what about that hurt is really causing you the most pain, you are able to move on from it. It may come instant and it may take longer like it did for me. But that's a step you can't forget. This could be the one thing that prevents you from ever feeling this way again. You know what you can and can't handle, so you will know what kind of man you can and can't be with the next time. This will be your inner alarm system the next time around. The one that went off before but you silenced it with fear of not wanting to be alone. But the alarm will only work if you turn it on. And before you can turn it on, you have to know it's there. So take some time and self-reflect on your past, or present, painful situations.

Look at how things ended in previous relationships and start to discover why. Be honest with yourself and even admit things you did that caused damage. Be honest with yourself. Write things down. Pray on them and be committed to never repeating the same behaviors again that caused you so much pain. Doing this will save you from future heartbreaks. This will definitely change the game for you.

Let it go!

Once you allow yourself to feel it and recognize what it is, your next step is to let it go! Although that may seem hard, it's the truth. Holding on to pain is like carrying around a large cage on your back every day. It's heavy, slows you down, and will eventually consume you if you let it. Harboring hurt is unhealthy and stops your growth in all areas of your life. You won't be the best mom, sister, daughter, or friend because you are not being the true you. Hurt stops you from being who God intended you to be. You won't allow yourself to love again because that cage will constantly be in the way between you and what you deserve.

You will begin to devalue yourself. You won't recognize your worth or potential to achieve success - which could affect your personal and professional life. You will second guess everything you do and question every thought before you could make it a reality. Holding on to hurt can literally affect every area of your life. Just think about how heavy that can be. You have entirely too much to do. And nothing will get done with hurt renting space in your head and in your heart.

How do you let it go? Great question! I can only give you the answer that worked for me. And that was through prayer. I prayed to God daily, throughout the day for peace. Was it hard? Yes! Did it happen right away? No! It took an extremely long time, but it happened. For a long time, I felt like God wasn't even listening to me. Like I had done something so bad that He was punishing me. I wanted that release to be instant, but it wasn't. It took some time. And it didn't happen until almost the end of my healing process. But I understood why later on. I had more work to do first and had some more challenges to overcome within, before I was able to really truly let it all go. But I did. I was able to let go of the pain, the anger I had toward him, and the disappointment I had within myself.

I know some of you may be thinking that prayer alone isn't going to fix anything. And you are right. I had to do work along with praying. I prayed daily the same prayer and cried out for God to make it better. And I had to change things within myself that allowed God to come in my situation to change it. And it was extremely hard because when you ask God to come and take over, He does just that. He begins to show you things about yourself and other people that you are not quite ready for. But when He does, listen and follow His lead. It will take you to exactly where you want to be. In perfect peace!

There are several things you can do alongside your prayers to get this process rolling. You must find a way to release what you are feeling in a healthy way. Whatever you decide to do my suggestion to you would be to do that thing consistently. Rather it is to pray, pray every day. If you write, write every day. If it's through song, sing your heart out daily. Whatever is your healthy release technique, have a routine to it. This will not only keep you on task, but it will also add some much needed consistency to your life. It gives you something to positively focus on besides the unthinkable. My healthy outlet was to write. I wrote my feelings in notes, poems and songs. However I needed to get it out, I did.

While I was praying daily, I was also writing. Every day I wrote a little in my phone of how I was feeling. I guess it was my personal diary. Every time my previous spouse and I had a fight, when I felt sad, when I was hurting or when I felt good that day, I wrote it out. It made me feel like I was taking control and talking to a friend at the same time. My memo pad was my friend. My listening ear. She knew everything and every emotion I was experiencing. And when I reviewed it, I realized that I had something more than my notes. I had a book. So that's where my first book, *Love on Fire* was birthed. It was all of my observations of what did or didn't happen in my marriage that could have made all the difference in us making things work.

You will be surprised what emotions will make you do. You have to turn your pain into passion and that passion will release you from the pain. My pain was released in two books, in addition to over thirty

> You have to find the one thing, or things, that helps you get a little of yourself back every day, and master it.

poems and songs. My peace came from my writings on my pain. I got it out and let it go. There is no way I could have imagined that. I let my feelings out a little every day and was consistent with it. It only takes fifteen to thirty minutes a day to focus on yourself and how you feel. It becomes very reflective and therapeutic at the same time. You have to find the one thing, or things, that helps you get a little of yourself back every day, and master it. You will soon feel a little lighter and a little freer every day. And then one day you will realize that you are experiencing the one thing that seemed so impossible to have again, peace.

Chapter 2
Forgiveness

The Pelican

The pelican was believed to pierce its own breast with its beak and feed its young of its blood. It symbolized Christ sacrificing himself for man forgiving all of our sins.

"Be even-tempered, content with second place, quick to forgive an offense. Forgive as quickly and completely as the Master forgave you". Colossians 3:13 MSG

"Make a clean break with all cutting, backbiting, profane talk. Be gentle with one another, sensitive. Forgive one another as quickly and thoroughly as God in Christ forgave you". Ephesians 4:31-32 MSG

Now that we have handled the pain, we can start rebuilding our lives. The only way to go is forward. You can't stay in the past. There is no room for growth there at all. We have to keep moving no matter how hard it is. And recognize that the harder it is, the greater the blessing once we get passed it. This is where we wipe our tears, pull our hair back into a ponytail, place the glasses on our face, and see things from another perspective. The perspective before was dark. Now let's add some light!

> *Now that we have handled the pain, we can start rebuilding our lives.*

Forgive yourself.

As women, because we handle so much we take the blame for things when they go wrong and the credit for when things go right. We wear ownership like it's a lamb skin leather jacket! This is especially true with our relationships. And often time after something happens in our relationships we internalize it all. We scratch our heads and ask those gut wrenching questions, "What did I do wrong?" "Is it the way I look?" "Was I really that much of a nag?" "Did I not do all the things he wanted me to do?" "Was I not pretty enough?" "What could I have done differently?" "What did I do to deserve this?" This list can go on and on with the what, when, why, and how's. We can ask ourselves any and everything but the answer to them all would be the same. "You are not to blame!" There is nothing you could have done to make or not make someone else hurt you. Rather the hurt was emotional, physical, or mental. None of it is your fault.

Blaming yourself or the other person doesn't solve the problem. It only generates more negative energy because you are now focusing on something totally irrelevant. That person whom you were in a relationship with had the choice to go left or go right. Nothing you could have done or said determined that choice. Nothing. So you have to let go of that thinking. Everyone born in this world was born with the wonderful gift called "Free Will". This gift gives everyone the power to make their own decisions and direct their own paths. It gives everyone the freedom to be the captain of their own ship. So we all make our own choices. It can be suggested that certain actions can influence someone else's decisions, but the final decision making is still theirs to make.

If you don't believe me, look into the very public relationships of the rich and famous. Some of our most beautiful and successful celebrities have been cheated on and some physically abused. They have money, the perfect figures, perfect hair, several homes, cars, diamonds, they have it all and yet they too are hurt. They also experience real life pains as we all do. They too are victims of another person's free will decision making. These people are perfect examples to show you that there is nothing anyone can do or have or say to prevent someone else from breaking your heart. So let's not play the blame game and focus on getting through this stage in our lives.

In order to truly get through a heartache, you have to forgive yourself. You can't carry that weight for someone else. Doing this lets the other person off too easy. While you are holding on to the pain they caused you, they are starting over. And how fair does that seem? It's not fair to you at all. You have to tell that bruised and beaten person on the inside of you that you are not the reason for this pain. This experience is not your fault. And even if it was, some things just happen. And even though it's hard to see the reason why, there is always a reason why. To find that out takes a lot of prayer, self-reflection, and honesty. It will take some time to figure out. But before that revelation can even occur, you have to forgive you.

I used to cry myself to sleep some nights thinking of my part in my heartbreak. I thought about my weight, since I had gained pounds after having two children. I would try diets, workout, and even try not to eat sometimes. I thought that if I had the body or shape like those women he cheated with that he would see me differently. That this would not happen to me again. He would have what he was looking for in me. But I was wrong. No matter how much I changed myself physically, he still would have done what he did. That was his decision to make and he made it a few times.

> Being hurt by him/them was/is not my fault! There is nothing I could have done to prevent this. I forgive myself!

I didn't stop with my weight or how I looked. I tormented myself almost every day reliving years of our relationship going over things I had said, done or didn't do. Wondering if I missed something. What was it that I missed?? What didn't I see that he was asking for that I didn't give? Why didn't I do something? I mean I went through every year, every month, every week, every day that we spent together wondering what the hell was my problem. I did this for years. And to be honest, I still think of this sometimes to this day. But I had to let it go. I finally realized that I had to stop blaming myself. No, I wasn't perfect and I did have some shortcomings but overall I was good to him. I was loyal, I was honest and I was loving. So I didn't do anything wrong in terms of making him break my heart. That was all his decision and it had nothing to do with me. It had everything to do with him. Once I realized that, and forgave myself for this entire situation, I felt a huge sense of relief.

I felt this relief a few years after my situation. But I want you to feel this relief now. If you don't learn anything else from this book, learn this. IT'S NOT YOUR FAULT!!! Forgive yourself and move on. There is nothing you could have done to prevent any of what was done to you. Accepting responsibility and taking ownership is two different things. You can accept responsibility for things you have done or said that was damaging to your relationship, but you can't own the entire failure of it. You can't blame yourself for someone else causing you physical, emotional, or mental harm. You just can't! So say this with me one good time, believe it and digest it! "Being hurt by him/them was/is not my fault! There is nothing I could have done to prevent this. I forgive myself!" And that's it!

Chapter 3
It's All About You !

Goose

Geese migration is symbolic of personal freedom and change. They enjoy their transition which typically attracts and leads other to follow in their direction.

"God, get me out of here, away from this evil; protect me from these vicious people. All they do is think up new ways to be bad; they spend their days plotting war games. They practice the sharp rhetoric of hate and hurt, speak venomous words that maim and kill".
Psalm 140: 1-3 MSG

"So let God work his will in you. Yell a loud no to the Devil and watch him scamper. Say a quiet yes to God and he'll be there in no time. Quit dabbling in sin. Purify your inner life".
James 4:8-10 MSG

If it's one thing heartbreak will do, it will teach you some things! It shows you what's important in your life, what matters to you, and how to move differently going forward. For me, the pain I felt with my ex was simultaneous with the hurt of my father's illness. The same weekend my father was diagnosed with terminal cancer was the same weekend I found out about all the offenses of my ex. Talk about double whammy. And during those two and half years I cared for my father, I was trying to rebuild my marriage. And when my father died, so did my marriage. So did everything I felt, held on to, or wanted. My heart wasn't just broken; it was shattered into a million pieces. I lost the two most important men in my life at the same time. Now the pain that this season in my life caused was indescribable. I still to this day can't quite put it in words to anyone so that they could truly understand. All I can say is it nearly destroyed me after it was all said and done. But almost is the key word. It didn't destroy me but made me better.

> But almost is the key word. It didn't destroy me but made me better.

Instead it taught me some things about myself and my life. It allowed me to see what was important and what wasn't. I started looking at everything in my life differently. I reevaluated friendships, business ideas, family, just everything. My entire world became different to me. I felt a few different ways. The one thing that was consistently felt by me during this time was positivity. I only wanted positive people with positive vibes around. I did not want anyone's negative thoughts, perceptions, notions, or energy around me. If you didn't make me happy or make me feel good, you had to go. And I still operate like that to this very day.

My tolerance for foolishness evolved to level zero. I no longer entertained negativity or false power from anyone. If you didn't love, respect, or care for me the way I did for you, I moved on without you. If you didn't uplift me, encourage, or support me, you didn't exist. If you didn't add value, increase, or magnify my life in anyway, you didn't matter. It may sound a little harsh but it's my truth. Eliminating those people and things in my life that caused any shape or form of negativity was the best thing that happened during my healing process. In some cases, I didn't have to remove some people, they removed themselves. Thank you God for those voluntary moves!!

Having people around you that smile when they see you, motivates you to keep going, or rejoiced when you're in their presence makes a world of difference in your life. I'm not much of a sports person, but it's just like any game. When a team sees fans in a crowd wearing their colors, screaming their name, chanting for them to do better, and rather they lose or win still stands by them, that team does amazing! They never give up! Win or lose they keep trying because they know that those fans in the crowd can see their victory even before they themselves can. Cheerleaders and fans make the difference at times in the overall success of a game. So having positive people in your life is just like that! Surround yourself with good people who only want the best for you each and every day. Get you a cheering section.

Once I had enough and realized my worth, everything changed. God blessed me with new friends, a new job, new business ventures, closer relationships with family and a

> *I was broken only to be rebuilt better.*

stronger relationship with Him. Clearing all of the negativity allowed me to hear Him and see Him clearly. Everything started to make sense. All of the "Ah-Ha" moments begin happening and I started understanding that all the pain I had experience didn't kill me, it made me better. But I wouldn't have realized that if I hadn't of removed all that that didn't matter. I was broken only to be rebuilt better. I'm a stronger, more optimistic, and loving version of myself. I understand my value and what God designed me to be. I understand my limits, desires, and gifts. I ultimately understand and now know my true worth. And when you know your worth, nothing or no one can take that from you. It becomes a standard and expectation of even more. Bigger. Better. Greater!

Date yourself!

Since I was an early teen, I realized that I have never really been alone. I always was in a relationship or had a special non-exclusive friend in between the relationships. I never spent time with myself. I put all my energy and time into making someone else happy, hoping to get the return. Every decision and move I made was for the satisfaction of a man. Deep right? Disney Movies sold me a dream. They gave me the perceptions that if I find a good man, everything will fall in place and I will live happily ever after. So that's what I did. I went out in search of the fairytale. And that search landed me in countless nightmares. But I had never looked at it that way. I looked at it from the perspective of love. I wanted and needed love. Not knowing that the real love I desired was in God showing me who I was. He needed to show me every great thing about myself so I could love myself. But I never left room for Him to show me this because my space was consumed with men. So after years of doing it my way, I'm finally trying it His way.

The first thing I did was pray of course. I prayed for God to develop a more intimate relationship with me so that I can experience His love first. And He kept telling me to be alone. Not to look or accept a date. And I wasn't so obedient. I felt strongly that I had been lonely in my marriage for so many years, that I wanted to not feel like that again once I was divorced. So I ignored His requests and went out a few times, and spoke on the phone with a couple of guys. But it never felt right. They would say or do something to upset or offend me. Especially when the topic of sex came up. And that let me know, I wasn't ready. God was right. I needed to be alone. So I was.

I started out making a date every Monday night for thirteen weeks at group counseling. This date was with a wonderful group therapy class I joined at a local church. There I shared my story and my heart with people who experienced the same thing and it was amazing. I was able to free my mind of misconceived thoughts of blame and shame from my broken marriage. I was able to reconnect with God because every class and assignment was derived from scriptures. I made new friends with people who added value to my life. I was able to stand alone and not feel lonely.

Then I would pray more. I started making more time for God. I remember having this time before I was with my previous spouse, but it was interrupted by life. But this time was a few minutes when I woke up, when I was in the car, listening to various sermons from various pastors, praying again when I was at work and again when I was ready to go to bed. I had to fill my mind, body, and soul with Him anyway I could. I'm not a holy roller or super religious, but I was able to praise and worship God every day, several times a day without completely changing my life. And eventually He completely changed my life. And in that routine, he healed me and made me whole again. I'm by no means perfect but I am better, stronger than I was when I first got divorced. And I owe that solely to God and how He pushed me to do better.

My next journey was to start having fun with myself. In this process I begin to figure out who I was exactly. I started to know what I liked and didn't like. Which is something that was smothered before with always worrying about what someone else wanted. I did simple things that made a huge impact in my life. Like going to a matinee alone, attending wine tastings and spending my lunch hours alone reading in a tea shop. I was able to do whatever I wanted whenever I wanted. I didn't have to consider anyone else or put someone else's wants before mine - which felt amazing. For once in my life, things were about me. And I was determined to take full advantage of this time.

I joined a gym to work out occasionally. (I'm definitely not a daily workout person!) Taking alone time allowed me to relieve stress, rest, have fun, and focus. I was able to hear things from God that I hadn't heard in a long time. My desires and prayers were coming to life because I removed all the negativity from my heart and allowed Him to work. I received blessings left and right. Things I was told no or it could never have happened, did. And that was only the beginning. Once I opened up my direct connection to God, we spoke often. He has probably been speaking to me all this time, but I couldn't hear Him over all the mess I had lived in for years. He has showed me if I do things, such as this book, my future would be amazing. I would receive more love and stability than ever before. I believe that, with making strides daily to achieve all of His blessings. I'm greedy so I want everything God has for me!

Closer to Him!

I know everyone reading this book may not be spiritual, but I am. So I have to speak to my truth and what's worked for me during my healing process. God has done miraculous things for me and directed me to share this with other women in my position. The major result of my healing process is the relationship I have developed with God. I am not religious but I am a spiritual woman believing, trusting, and loving God. I know without Him I could not have picked up the pieces of my broken heart and rebuilt it in a better form. He gets all glory for that. And this is how He did it.

I grew up in church going faithfully every Sunday with my family. My father knew the Word by heart and was able to apply it to every situation we experienced as a family, good or bad. So in my adulthood, it was only expected that I continue the same faith. And I did. Even getting closer to Him by attending church events, retreats, and attending Bible study weekly. I learned how to pray and how to declare things unto God. I wasn't perfect and didn't know everything, but I had a pretty good idea of God and my role with Him. I had a praying routine and special dedicated times with God daily. But this life changed when I met my husband. He didn't do anything to change my life, but he didn't do anything to add to it either.

By the time I met my husband I was twenty-five. But before meeting him I'd always known that I would, one day, be in a long term relationship that would lead to marriage. Before meeting my previous spouse I had been in a long term relationship that had ended. Shortly after that I began entertaining male friends that I would spend time with occasionally just to fill the void of being alone. Although this was the life of a typical twenty-five-year-old, it wasn't what I wanted for myself. Growing up in a strong family structure that was my heart's desire. I wanted a husband, children, and a family to call my own. Because I was entertaining situations that were going nowhere, for a short second I didn't see marriage in my future anymore. So I did what I knew to do, pray! I prayed for a husband and wrote everything I wanted him to be in a letter to God. I actually had about forty different skills, characteristics and values in this letter that I prayed over and placed in my Bible for safe keeping. I told God if He blessed me with this amazing man, that I would be the happiest girl in the world. And six months later that's exactly what He did.

After a few months of dating my husband, I reviewed my list and noticed that he exhibited all but one of my requirements to God. So I was ecstatic. I knew in my bones that this man was it. God gave me exactly what I asked for and more. And when we exchanged our first I love yous, it just made it that much clearer to me. I felt great! Like a kid in a candy store with an endless amount of money. He made me feel happy, safe, desired, and loved all the time. So I spent all the extra time I had with him. My time with him increased daily without noticing the one on one time I had with God started to decreased. I still went to church, but I didn't pray the same for a few reasons. One, I was so wrapped up in my husband that I forgot. Two, he didn't really go to church or pray so I didn't want to seem like a "goodie two shoe". Three, since he was practically everything I asked for, I felt like I didn't need to ask God for anything else. I was good. But looking back on it now, this is where things went left for me.

I used to ask my husband to attend church with me sometimes, but there was always an excuse. So I just let it go. I figured I would just be the spiritual one in the house and save him on my own. Even after we married, I can count on one hand how many services he attended with me. I stopped going to Bible study and I stopped my involvement with church because I wanted to be with him anytime he was available. Although at the time, I thought I was just being a good girlfriend and a loyal wife, I didn't realize that I altered my entire life just for him. He never asked me to or told me this was necessary. I just did it for the sake of not being without him. Not understanding that if he wanted to be with me, we should have been able to meet in the middle.

Once things started going really bad in our marriage I couldn't understand why. Why me? Why my marriage? I did everything the right way and did everything asked of me. So why do I have these problems. But it wasn't until I separated from my husband and went on ice that God revealed some answers to my questions. What He told me was that I put this man before Him. I moved Him out of his rightful first place and made Him last. I stopped seeking Him and stopped having that alone time daily. Without that alone time, I couldn't hear Him. I couldn't hear Him clearly tell me that I was making bad decisions, or that what I thought was real was not. I couldn't hear His directions nor see His signs. I was blocked and so was my vision. No one did that to me but me. I altered my intimate relationship with God, who treated me like a queen, for an intimate relationship with a man who didn't even see me as valuable enough to keep in his royal court.

Once I got that revelation I felt horrible. I was mad at myself. Although my husband made some mistakes and did indeed hurt me, some of them were my fault due to me severing the relationship I had with God. That's when He told me about going on ice and being alone. He expressed to me that I didn't spend enough time on my own dealing with myself. I went from relationship, to situation, to relationship just to avoid being alone. When being alone at times was exactly what I needed. If I had of spent that time alone with Him, most of the heartbreaks I experienced would not have even happened. I would have been sharper and wiser. I would know myself and all the things I needed or truly wanted. I would have been more confident and assure of myself. I would have been complete. Being complete and happy would have attracted the right people who were in that same lane or higher. But broken people attract broken people, so that explains everything and every relationship I have ever experienced.

Taking some time away and reconnecting with God helped me so much. He allowed me to see past my pain and into what was really causing me so much misery. This was beneficial because now I know exactly what to do and what to look for in my next relationship. I know what really matters to me and I'm confident in expressing my values. I know the standards I have to stand on and what I need. I know that a relationship with God is essential in the next man I am involved with. There is so much that has been revealed to me after I reconnected with God. So I am more than confident that my next time around will be better than great. It will be abundant, just like He wanted for me this entire time. So I'm beyond hopeful, I'm excited!!!

Chapter 4
Take Out the Trash

Vulture

Vultures have been viewed as a bird that enjoys death. Some feel that the bird shift death to life, making old things new again. This is why it symbolizes the act of cleansing, renewal, and transformation.

"Forget about what's happened, don't keep going over old history. Be alert, be present. I'm about to do something brand-new. It's bursting out! Don't you see it? There it is. I'm making a road through the dessert, rivers in the badlands".
Isaiah 43:18-19 MSG

"But those who trust in the Lord for help will find their strength renewed. They will rise on wings like eagles; they

*will run and not get weary; they will walk and not grow
weak." Isaiah 40:31 GNT*

After my marriage ended, I started evaluating every
relationship that I have ever been in. And I realized a few
things. I had a few patterns or similarities that I experienced
in each relationship. I have experienced men who created
children outside of our relationships, men who blatantly lied
and disrespected me in various ways. One thing that
became clear is that I either voluntarily or involuntary shared
some men I was involved with. What do I mean by that? Well
either I was cheated on and didn't know that it wasn't just me
or I knew I wasn't the only one and accepted an
arrangement for the time being. To my current knowledge, I
have only dated two men that have never cheated on me.
Although infidelity didn't occur, those relationships dissolved
for different reasons.

Outside of those two men, all of my other relationships
uncovered two patterns. Realizing these patterns changed
my view of, not only, relationships, but of me. One pattern
was that I confused sex with love and the other was that I
remained in unhealthy relationships for the sake of
consistency. Revelation of these patterns hit me hard. I
couldn't believe what I had done and allowed to repeatedly

happen in my life. I couldn't figure it out. I was raised by my dad so I didn't have daddy issues. I have a loving mother so I was raised strong. I grew up in church so I had values and beliefs. I have two master degrees so I'm clearly educated. And I have eight siblings so I wasn't lonely. So what was the problem?

The answer was nothing. I was just young and living life with no specific goal in mind regarding relationships. I just wanted a relationship. I wanted to feel love and would allow anything to have it. I let my heart lead me where my head should have known better than to go. I love hard. I'm in love with love. So any feeling or part of love was what I craved and wanted to hold on to. I own these mistakes and don't blame any of the men of these previous relationships for anything. I made my own decisions to stay involved with these men knowing they weren't good for me. The only way I could guarantee that I didn't make these same mistakes again was to truly dive into these patterns and understand why I accepted them as normal in the first place.

> I let my heart lead me where my head should have known better than to go.

Sex ain't love, honey!

My first relationship was with my elementary and high school sweetheart. He was my first crush, my first kiss, my first everything! You couldn't tell me anything wrong or bad about this boy. I was coo-coo for cocoa puffs over him. He used to tell me he loved me, I was smart and beautiful, I deserved the world and he would give it to me when we got older. As funny as it sounds writing this now, I truly believed that he would. So when he suggested sex and where it would take our relationship I didn't hesitate. I thought we were in love and would be together forever. What harm could it do? It did plenty. The dynamics of our relationship was never the same after that. Bad decisions and mistakes were made because of that very thing called sex.

No matter how many fights or disagreements we had, sex with him made me feel loved. That's when he was focused on me and gave me all of his attention. Being young I didn't know that it was wrong and my so called love was based on a false pretense. But it was. So everyman after that, is what I looked for again. I knew what they all wanted and figured if I gave it to them, they would give me love. Some was love and some was pure lust. I always felt convicted after performing the act itself but I kept doing it because it was the norm. It was what was expected. I went from one relationship to the next looking for something they could never give me, which was real love.

Sure, things felt great and the passion was amazing at the time. But as soon as that event was over, so was the love. There is no other feeling more awful than sharing your body with someone and then they get up and leave like nothing was special about it. And then to find out that they did the same thing recently with someone else. Furthermore, proving that nothing was special about it or you at all. That feeling and realization is beyond painful. It's extremely embarrassing and is a feeling I don't wish on any young woman. Clearly then although I had high self-esteem, I didn't love myself or know what love truly was. But after recognizing this very thing and developing a closer relationship with God, that is no longer my reality. I know, have, and give real love because of Him. So I can firmly say that I will never make that mistake again. Never.

Follow the expiration dates!

I'm huge on paying attention to the expiration dates on food labels. They are there for a reason. These dates are there to warn you that it's time to throw something out before it starts stinking, changing colors, and could make you ill if consumed. I throw out or use foods the day or two before the date to avoid any of those things from happening. So if I'm

45

so good with this with my food, why couldn't I recognize the same thing in my relationships? Some of those definitely lasted way beyond their expiration date but I didn't throw them out!

This brings me to my second pattern that I recognized. In my relationships I had the willingness to stay in them just to have a consistent someone always there. They were essentially place fillers or card holders. I did everything I could to hold on to them when I should have been saying goodbye. I was trying to fix things and make it all work. Allowing men to have children on me and forgive them so easily. Knowing that I wasn't the only women in their lives and unofficially signing off on sharing them. Allowing them to verbally abuse me and diminish my gifts. I did this. I allowed this all for the sake of love. All for the sake of having someone, anyone besides being alone. I would rather have consistency over happiness. I didn't realize this until I allowed God to show me where I went wrong in my past.

This was very clear in my marriage. I could have left the moment I found out that everything I thought I knew was a lie. But remember, this was the same time I found out about my dad. I felt like my dad could leave me at any moment, any day with his illness that I had no control over. But my marriage at the time I did control. My husband wanted me to stay so I did. Not because I loved him so much and that I had gotten over everything so fast, but because he offered consistency. I needed something stable to hold me in place on the outside, while I was falling apart on the inside. My dad was my best friend and purest form of love felt before my children. So to keep my marriage in tact while dealing with his health problems seemed liked the smartest thing to do.

But this proved to be the wrong decision. I never dealt with my pain that my previous spouse caused me because I was dealing with my dad. So every small problem we had during those two years became bigger than needed. Nothing was ever good enough nor right. I blew things out of proportion and sometimes was irritated enough to initiate fights. I was angry on the inside because he had hurt me so badly and wouldn't acknowledge it. I couldn't see passed anything because I had dealt with nothing. Because I pushed my feelings down deep, I developed a resentment for him that was strong. A lot of it was his unwillingness to take ownership in his part, but a lot was me as well. I couldn't deal with two dying relationships at the same time so I focused on the most important one - and that was Daddy.

I couldn't figure out why God would allow me to experience this great of two pains at the same time. The average person doesn't have to deal with all that at one time.

> *So I consider myself God's very own disco ball. He broke me many time and in many ways, but only to create His works in me.*

That's two major life events happening at the same exact moment. Why did I have to lose both of them together? I didn't know what He was punishing me for but I knew I was surely being punished for something. It wasn't until I began healing that the answer was revealed to me. God needed me broken completely in order to build me back up better. Stronger. Wiser. Happier. God knew that as strong as I was, I could have handled both situations on my own at different times. But to experience both simultaneously, I was destroyed. And being destroyed made me depend on Him more. He brought me back to Him, which I should have never left in the first place.

My faith grew. My prayer life changed. I began fasting. I learned how to speak to my Angels and ask for their help daily. I trusted God more than ever. And it was only because in all of the pieces my heart was in, God put each one of them back together slowly. But the refurbished product is so much better than the old one. My heart, soul, and life have been restored! I heard a woman say once that a disco ball is so beautiful because its glass was broken a million time before it was a finished product. So I consider myself God's very own disco ball. He broke me many times and in many ways, but only to create His works in me. So although this was the toughest season I have ever experienced, I know it won't be the last. He is going to continually refine me until I'm right - perfect.

Chapter 5
Soul Ties Are Very Real

Albatross

The word albatross is sometimes used metaphorically to mean a psychological burden that feels like a curse. In a poem entitled, "The Rime of the Ancient Mariner", this blackbird is referenced for possessing a dead sailor's soul.

"For our struggle is not against flesh and blood, but against the rulers, against the authorities, against the powers of this dark world and against the spiritual forces of evil in the heavenly realms. Therefore, put on the full armor of God, so that when the day of evil comes, you may be able to stand your ground, and after you have done everything, to stand."
Ephesians 6:12-13 NIV

"Don't become partners with those who reject God. How can you make a partnership out of right and wrong? That's not partnership; that's war." 2 Corinthians 6: 14-15 MSG

Imagine that you have a crayon in your hand and then break it in half. Now you look at the break. It's not smooth or perfect. It's rigid and uneven. Sometimes one side is longer than the other leaving one side heavy carrying all the weight. It sounds simplistic but this is literally what happens when relationships end. They start off whole, full of color, and the perfect shape. But then a break happens, causing more harm than good for one side. One side may still be considered cute and be used in future art works. But the other is left missing its half that has moved on. This half is typically smaller and considered not so cute to use anymore. But just because the color isn't being used doesn't mean that it can't still be effective. The question is how does it work? What can be done to make this side useful again? This same concept can be used when explaining soul ties that linger after breakups.

When we break up with someone who we have been intimate with, physically they are gone but a part of them is still there. Sometimes it never goes away because we don't know exactly what it is. We think it must be love or maybe I shouldn't have broken up with them. Although those are real possibilities, majority of the time that is false. If your inner self spoke loud enough to say good bye to someone, it was for a sincere reason. But majority of the time it's because we have made a strong imprint on that person's soul through sexual relations. What we have created with that person is a soul tie.

That soul tie was intentionally meant to be created for our soul mates. The one we were supposed to be with forever. But unfortunately, we don't quite live by those ideas anymore. We make our own decisions of who we will share our bodies with, sometimes not even wanting to be with that person forever. And that's okay. That's how life was for me as well so I'm definitely not judging. But after so many years of various relationships with men who shattered my heart, I begin to reevaluate how I viewed sex. And through self-evaluation, I begin to learn more of what exactly soul ties were, how to get rid of them, and how they affected me personally from relationship to relationship.

I have been an active participant in at least five long term relationships before I met my previous spouse. I've always prided myself on that number because I felt it made me rare and special. I loved love and loved it hard. When I was with you, I was there for the long haul. I was loyal, faithful, and considered you to be the number one priority. But after my divorce, God allowed me to see myself in every past relationship I was in at-a-glance. He showed me where I went wrong and where those I trusted with my heart had failed me. And the main thing He revealed to me involved sex and the affects it left on me.

> *I shared myself with men I should not have. I gave them a piece of me that I can't get back.*

Every relationship I was involved in, for the most part was sexual. I was never pressured into sex; it was just something that was considered typical in a relationship. At least that's what I thought. Being connected to someone that I loved (or thought I loved) was magnificent to me. I loved being wanted and enjoyed being desired. But little did I know, that was the start of all of my relationship problems. I shared myself with men I should not have. I gave them a piece of me that I can't get back. And they weren't appreciative nor deserving. They didn't see the value in my soul tie or my worth. So when it was all said and done, it was literally a waste of sin. I went against everything I was raised to believe for men who didn't add any value to my life. To make my heavenly father hurt, I should have at least gotten something out of it but I didn't.

Having premarital sex caused me a lot of pain and heartache. It kept men in my life, who were supposed to be a season, way passed their expiration date. It gave me a false sense of security, love, and respect. These men didn't love me like I thought. If they did, it wouldn't have been another man after them. Those sexual encounters were just fleshly mistakes that caused years of pain and wasted a lot of my time I can never get back. I regret so much but can't harbor on it. I've learned from it. It was my free will decisions to make and now I know not to make again. Now that I know my true worth, what I want and what I need, I have a different focus. God has revealed to me that He will make up to me every hurt I've felt before by men. He has already restored me to feel whole again. So that will make all the difference in the next relationship I'm involved in. That relationship will be a bonus to my happiness because I won't be dependent upon it for internal joy. God has already given me that.

While in this revelation, one thing that I learned was that I had taken my soul tie from each man with me to the next. Which is why I was always in bondage worrying about them, why they did what they did to me and why couldn't they see my greatness. I couldn't get over it. I couldn't move on. So the feelings of hurt and rejection I felt from one man, I took with me in the relationship I had with the next. This caused me to surrender and repeat the same experiences over and over again with each man. They were all the same spirit but with a different face. This is what I attracted because I didn't have the knowledge to know what I had on my spirit. The heaviness of rejection, fear, sadness, and desperation was on me but it was dressed up with a smile and pretty face. But that vulnerable energy in me attracted controlling energy in the men I was dating. Which was my experience so many times.

Men who control do it to women who allow them to. We don't stand up or voice what we think is right. So they overpower us with authority and lack of respect. They don't feel accountable to anyone because they are all powerful. They make their own decisions without considering you at all. That's why it's so easy for them to cheat, because that's a choice they made and no one can stop them. That's why when they do cheat, an apology never comes first. A blanket reason statement is given to cover up their indiscretions. You can either choose to accept it or not. It doesn't mean one thing to them what you decide. Regardless they will be good. And if you do accept them back, more likely than not, they will do it again because they know you have given them power.

My God, if You had only shown me this stuff before, I would have done things so differently. But these were things I created by not waiting to have sexual relations. So I blame no one but myself. But God showed me how to completely get out from my own mistakes. I had to pray them off. I had to forgive every man I had ever been with for everything thing they did to me. And once I forgave them, I had to intentionally pray for God to release the soul tie they had on me. I needed Him to remove every connection I made or imprint they left on my soul, my body, and my mind. This was a repeated prayer and very heartfelt because the more I thought of it, the more hurt was pulled from me. Breaking off from a soul tie is no easy task. You will feel every bit of that thing remove itself from you. You will feel the lust, the hurt, the pain, the sadness, and power be released from you, one tie at a time. It won't be pretty at all but it will become beautiful once it is complete.

But praying for your soul ties from your previous relationships won't be the end of it. I learned this the hard way. Even though you are now free and feeling good you are not done. You will start getting phone calls and texts from those previous relationships wanting to come back. They will be on you heavy. This is nothing we haven't experienced before. It's like the old saying, they never miss you until you are gone. It's more like, that other tie is missing the control from the other side. It convinces them to reconnect and see what happens. But you have to be strong and know that this has to end. And the way to end it is to now pray for your soul tie to be broken off of them. Now you have to be intentional about praying for their release. This will allow them freedom and to release you completely from their spirit. And once that happens, the ties are completely broken and you can be free to be you again. Out of bondage.

I didn't experience or understand this entire subject until I went through my divorce. I was worrying about where he was, who he was with, and what he was doing and I couldn't shake it. I was always sad, hurt, disgusted and devastated that the man I gave my entire life to didn't want me anymore. And that's when God started to work with me. He revealed some ugly things about myself but they were necessary for me to see. This will prevent me from ever doing things the same the next time love presents itself to me. So I encourage you to be ready because this process won't be easy but it will be beneficial for the next stage in your life. Freedom.

Chapter 6
Protect Your Jewel

Falcon

Falcons never rest. They never close their eyes, even when they are sleeping. To many, they are seen as a protective guardian by nature.

"Flee from sexual immorality. All other sins a person commits are outside the body, but whoever sins sexually, sins against their own body. Do you not know that your bodies are temples of the Holy Spirit, who is in you, whom you have received from God? You are not your own; you were bought at a price. Therefore, honor God with your bodies." 1 Corinthians 6:18-20 NIV

"A wife of noble character who can find? She is worth far more than rubies, her husband has full confidence in her and lacks nothing of value." Proverbs 31: 10-12 NIV

Let me start this chapter off by saying this, nothing I'm about to say is judgment. I am new to this kept and sacred life. I never wanted or tried to even be celibate before this season. I didn't see a point in trying. I knew if I was in a relationship, that was expected and required. So why waste my time. So believe me when I say I know, I sound crazy now suggesting this for you. But give me a chance to explain further and maybe you can see things differently like I did.

Together so far, we have been through so much during this healing process. We relived the past, learned mistakes made, forgiven ourselves and those who hurt us, and even broken off soul ties. We've learned that sex is not love and when engaged with the wrong person it can cause more harm than good. But let me take it to another step with you. So after all that, who wants to repeat these steps ever again? No one I'm sure. No one wants to feel void, hurt, abandoned, and used several times. No one wants to keep praying and fighting off negative soul ties. No one wants to keep investing energy in

No one wants to keep investing energy in men who don't want to invest anything in return.

men who don't want to invest anything in return. This I know for a fact. So what do we need to do differently now in order to not repeat history? There are so many answers to this question, but the one I'm going to address in this chapter is celibacy.

The Merriam-Webster's Dictionary definition of celibacy is: the state of not being married and abstention from sexual intercourse. The Urban Dictionary defines it as: having no sex whatsoever; usually as a part of a religious vow even though not many religions practice it.

Now let me give you my definition of it: A personal vow made between you and God in efforts to protect your most precious jewel, protect your heart, protect your soul, protect yourself respect, protect your value, and to protect your future.

This concept is new to me and came about after my divorce. I've been with my previous spouse for ten years and was comfortable not having to share myself with anyone but him. I remember being asked by my single friends after I got married what was the biggest difference I had noticed so far. And my response was always that my conviction from having premarital sex was gone. I always knew what I was doing was wrong but I never considered not doing it either for the sake of maintaining a relationship. I knew that any man I was with expected and wanted me to have sex with them and the thought of not wasn't a consideration. SO being married took that stress off me and made me feel like finally I was doing something right in God's eyes. But I didn't know that this feeling of peace would be short lived by the dissolution of my marriage.

Not being married anymore gave me freedom from hurt but also created in me a new sense of anxiety. I didn't feel safe or protected anymore being single. I didn't feel that covering from someone who loved me and whose responsibility was to shield me from all things. Once we initially separated I remember thinking, "Now I have to share myself with someone else when I thought I would never have to do that again." That thought alone hurt and frightened me because I worried about all things that came with dating and sex. Things such as diseases, pregnancies, and even rape if I was ever to say no to the wrong person. It made me extremely insecure and very uncomfortable. It was so beyond unsettling.

Once those feelings came over me I began thinking of other experiences that my marriage rescued me from when I was dating. Marriage protected me from being involved with a man that went home immediately after having sex because what he wanted he received and had no other reason to stay. Or from a man whose lips I've kissed that tasted like the woman from another day. Or from the man who never wanted to kiss at all because kissing created feelings that he wasn't ready to be responsible for or handle. Marriage rescued me from men who never wanted to strive toward real love but instead just want my body anyway that they desired. Marriage saved me in so many ways. It made me feel as if my life of experiencing broken promises, undeveloped love, mishandled emotions, and immoral physical contact with men who didn't have a genuine investment in me were over. But there I was back in that fishbowl full of disappointment again.

I remembered dating and having feelings of being used, played, and misled often. I started to devalue myself and think that maybe I deserved being treated this way. Or even that this is the way it's supposed to be and just accept it. I began acting like nothing was wrong on the outside but inside nothing was ever right. That created a tender and exposed feeling in the middle of my chest that developed from years of never being taken care of properly. I didn't look at men the same way and started trying to play the game like they did. And this mentality turned into even more pain and more hurt because no matter how hard we try, women just don't operate like men. Nothing seemed to be working and everything I thought I had a grip on began slipping away.

I know my experiences and emotions sound familiar. And it's unfortunate because we make these quick and premature decisions on relationships that don't have our best interest from inception. So you are probably saying right about now, "So what should I do differently? How can I stop this from happening again and regain control over my life?" It's a hard and simple answer all at the same time. Protect yourself by protecting your jewel. Stop sharing something so precious with men who don't care, understand, or know your worth. Don't lie with another man who is only going to take from you and add no value to your life. Stop. It hasn't gotten you anywhere this far, and it won't take you any further later. Am I really saying that this is going to fix all of your dating problems? Yes, and No. No it won't help you make better decisions unless you are ready for it. Taking a vow of celibacy is hard and sincere. You have to understand why you are doing it, how to do it, and what you expect from

> *This is not a control measure for your relationships that forces men to commit. This is about you and your worth.*

it. This is not a control measure for your relationships that forces men to commit. This is about you and your worth. It has nothing to do with anyone else.

Once you figure that out then, yes, this will surely help you make better decisions about the next man or men you date. How? A few different ways. One thing that having sex early in a relationship does is expedite the natural development of a meaningful connection. This can cause underdevelopment or premature emotions. When you are dating someone, it's all fun and exciting in the beginning. Everything seems so perfect. You are so smitten by the newness of it all that you may ignore warning signs that something may need to be addressed. But when you add sex to the mix, it makes you feel connected, in strong feelings or even in love with that other person before you actually get to know them. You are more attached to the good feelings that sex brings than the person themselves. The problem this poses is that the "get to know you" portion of the relationship was skipped. You didn't have a chance to find out anything substantial about that person before this intimate connection was made.

Yeah, you know the basics and maybe even a little about his family. But do you know how he handles conflict? How he views spirituality? What he thinks about family and building one together? When you cry, how does he respond? Or can he even handle your emotions with care? Does he know that something happened in your childhood that makes you react a certain way? Or how your relationship is with your parents or guardians? Does he know your personal desires and wants? Does he take care of his children in a way that you would want him to take care of yours? Is he stable physically and emotionally? Is he holding anything back from you now that could deter your entire life? All of these questions are typically things we don't find out about someone until something bad happens. And it usually happens right after having a sexual relationship. Then you wonder why did he say that to me in an argument? Or how could he react like that and not care about how that would make me feel? And you realize that you don't like this character at all, but you are so attached to the sex that you remain.

If you take the time to slow down and get to know the men you date, all of the important questions can be answered for you both. And if you decide to end the relationship after careful review, then you can do so without all the drama that's inevitable after a sexual connection has been made. You are less likely to waste time deciding about the physical feeling you could be missing if they left, and concern yourself more on the emotional feeling you can gain in a better partner later. Time gives you so many valuable things. Things that you deserve and should have without question. It presents you with an opportunity to learn things about your mate, but also about yourself. I've learned the hard way that you can't expect a man to understand you if you don't understand yourself. You have to know your essential needs and wants. You have to know your likes and dislikes. No one else can give you that but you. And you can learn those things by reflecting on previous relationships and remembering what hurt you or made you happy. And those are things you avoid and search for in the next man.

This journey to remain celibate is not an easy one by far. It's extremely hard. But that's why you need help. And there is no greater help than God. Ask Him to reveal to you his plan for your life and to keep you on His guided path. Ask Him for understanding, strength, and power. He will tell you. He will begin with letting you know that He created you more precious than any earthly jewel. He designed you with a purpose and designed you perfectly. He gave you superpowers with the gift of carrying and delivering life into this world. You are guardian of generations. His entire world is created inside of you. His love for you is different from that very concept alone. That's why you are so precious and should be handled with care.

You are a royal princess because your heavenly father is a King. In this world disrespecting a princess is a crime with various punishments. So what makes you think you are any less respectable? Your Father is not just any King, but the only King. King of all Kings. Because of Him we are all royalty and should start acting as such. Especially us women. Our value, worth, and power is beyond our understanding. Which is why we do the things we have in the past because we didn't know. But now that we do, how will things be different? Understanding this and refusing to be treated the way I have in my past is what shifted my thinking. Something that I always thought was a ridiculous concept in my past, is now genius to me. It's not easy by far. Especially when you meet great men who don't share that same vision. But no matter how great he may seem, the one God has that is in alignment with you will be even greater.

This will be a tough journey to begin for those who are interested. So I've listed some quick tips to help you along the way. These are things that are helping me currently and I'm praying they help you as well.

1. **Avoid Seductive Music**: Thinking about engaging in sexual activities is what gets you into trouble. So stop thinking about it. A way to do that is to not listen to sexually suggestive music and

watching explicit television and movies. You will be vulnerable in the beginning of this lifestyle change so what you see and hear are very crucial. There are plenty of other forms of entertainment that will make you happy.

2. **Enjoy Life**: My Pastor told us singles that in order to have a kept lifestyle you have to first get a life! It's easy to engage in certain behaviors when you are bored. That's how random text message and inbox conversations start. And before you know it, your doorbell is ringing. So go out and try new things and have a good time. Take that class you've always wanted to but didn't have time to. Workout and stay fit in the outdoors. Do whatever you need to in order to have a full life without sex.

3. **Get out of bed**: Use your bed for sleeping only. Don't lounge around and think about things. The bed itself can create memories or desires that encourage you to call up your exes. If you are home, get up and go in the living room space to watch television.

4. **Find a Kept Support Group**: Try to find more people who are on the celibate path as well. This

creates comfort, safety, guidance, and support for you during this time. You would be surprised at how much support there is around you. I joined a virtual community of women who value themselves and what they have to offer. Prayers, scriptures and real conversations occur during this group communication to assist in this new lifestyle. Just search and ask, and you will definitely find what you need.

5. **Pray**: Have a real conversation with God about sex and your thoughts. It's not like He doesn't already know anyway. But tell him how you feel, what you think and how you need Him so that you can stay focus. This is just as you would do in any fasting period. Ask Him for strength to get you through.

I know this will be hard and sounds like a foreign language to some of you. I understand it because that was me. It's still me. So don't feel bad and know there is no judgment here at all. Even if you are not ready today to start this new life. I whole heartedly understand and respect your decision. I just want you to know that if you have experienced any of the things I've discussed in this chapter, then this is the only way to protect your heart, soul, and mind from being broken like it has been so many times in the past. Choosing a life of celibacy isn't a prison sentence or any other form of punishment. It's not you controlling your relationship nor should be used as a measure to force marriage. It's a way for you to get to learn yourself, your worth, and your purpose.

And if you do try it and fail, don't condemn yourself. Keep trying until you get it right. God won't leave you or be upset with you for your mistakes. It's your genuine efforts that he loves most. SO every time you fall, know that Daddy Jesus will be right there to pick you up and help you start again. It's a tough journey but what you will find at the end of it will be greater than you've ever imagined. The one you will be with in the end will genuinely love you and the person you are, and not what you can do for them.

Chapter 7
Glow Up After Your Break Up

Crow

Crows are not our most favorable birds but according to American Indians, this bird represents creativity. They exemplify power, intelligence, courage, determination, and flexibility for what they want.

"And don't for a minute let this Book of the Revelation be out of mind. Ponder and meditate on it day and night, making sure you practice everything written in it. Then you'll get where you're going; then you'll succeed. Haven't I commanded you? Strength! Courage! Don't be timid; don't get discouraged. God, your God, is with you every step you take. "Joshua 1:8-9 MSG

"Isaac planted crops in that land and took in a huge harvest. God blessed him. The man got richer and richer by the day until he was very wealthy". Genesis 26:12 MSG

Have you ever thought about how much time, attention, dedication, and money we put into our relationships with men? Just think about how much you invest in another person making sure that they are happy, comfortable, and satisfied. How much you change your plans, make arrangements to be a support, plan events to show love and listen to them talk about things you may or may not care about. Think hard. Especially reflecting on relationships that lasted more than six months. And now think about what you are left with once the relationship ends. Outside of children, what benefit did that person really leave in your life? I'm sure majority of the relationships we can remember left us with nothing. Nothing but heartache, pain, and stress. Now imagine if you would have invested that same amount of efforts into yourself, into building a business or improving your career. The returns on your personal development would have left you in a much greater position emotionally, spiritually, and financially in six months or less. Now it's your time to do that. And let me show you how.

Pain into passion.

When I was initially going through a rough season in my life everything around me was failing. All at one time, I lost a job I loved, my dad was terminally diagnosed, my marriage was beyond strained, and my daughter was only three months old. I experienced a small form of postpartum depression that didn't shift toward my daughter but toward my previous spouse. God blessed me with a job month later but it was a job I absolutely hated. I loved the people I worked with and the service I provided to my clients, but I wasn't respected, challenged, or supported. I was trapped in a cubicle that I covered in scriptures. I even blessed my cubicle entrance with holy oil as if it was garlic waring off vampires. I didn't want anyone who did not resemble God and his heart to come near me.

To say I was in a bad place was an understatement. I was in what I thought was the lowest point in my life. I was broken in every form of the way. My emotions were shattered, my heart was crushed, anxiety was intense, and fears were heightened. I couldn't understand it. I typically did everything right. I was a loyal wife, great mother, good friend, stellar employee, and a faithful Christian. I tithed, gave in offering, and went to church every Sunday like clockwork. So why was this happening to me? Why was I going through such a hard time in my life? And as I prayed and prayed, one night God said to me as clear as the sky, "Why not you?" And there it was. An answer that I had to meditate on, pray on, and live with. And I did.

I trusted God that this was a season that I must go through in order to get to my next level. This hard time was mine and was for me and only me. God had to break me in order to make me better. There were things I had to learn and experience before I could make it to the other side. And I say God broke me because He did. Because I believe that He is the Master of everything, He allowed those experiences to happen to me. He gave permission for assignments knowing that I would pass them. He wouldn't put more on my than I can bare and I did in His perfect will. Because of that realization I changed my perspective. My situations didn't change but how I handled those situations did. And this is how.

First, I increased my prayer life. I prayed every morning, on the train, walking down the street, entering the building of the job I hated, and when I got to my cubicle. And when I sat down at my desk I read a daily devotional and scriptures of the day faithfully for encouragement and support. I prayed walking around the building and throughout the day. I thanked God on my commute home, back on the train, walking to my car, and once I walked in the door at home. I prayed before I went to bed and was prepared to repeat my endeavors every day for two and half years.

Then I accepted my assignment. I knew that the job that I hated so much was for a reason. And the reason was unclear to me at first but that's because I had a job to do. I had an assignment to complete. So I did. I told God, coworkers, friends, and whoever would ask me that I was only there for a short time. That I would be there until my assignment was complete and God saw fit to release me. And some understood what I meant but others thought I was crazy. It didn't matter to me. Either way, I continued on with this in mind. I worked that job with integrity, respect and honor even when the same wasn't given to me. I treated each client like the child of God they were and poured my all into serving them with excellence. This was a challenge but also a pleasure for me. Although I hated coming there every day no one I worked with or worked for deserved to feel or hear that disdain. They deserved to be treated with respect and given love, and that is what I did. Which is why I've made lifelong friends with some of my previous coworkers.

Then I started to attend church events and workshops more. I wanted to surround myself with spiritual people and engage in spiritual encounters anyway I could. I stayed away from the marriage events because it just didn't make sense being there without my husband. And the women's events seemed more geared toward seasoned sisters. But I didn't let that stop me from searching. There were so many options that my church presented to us but the one that caught my eye was an entrepreneurship seminar. The flyer wasn't attractive or pretty, but the wording about being your own boss and developing your God given talents caught my attention. At the first event one of the speakers said a coin phrase that hasn't left my spirit yet. He said that God has given all of us talents and skills that can generate income today. And one of them is pain. We have to learn how to turn our pain into passion letting the passion turn into profit.

> *...when you go through something when you go through something successfully, God wants you to help someone else get through that same thing.*

What that gentleman was essentially saying was that when you go through something successfully, God wants you to help someone else get through that same thing. And where there is a genuine and transparent experience available for others to use as a tool, they will pay for it. That thing hit me hard. How can I do that? What was my pain right now that I could see as profitable? My pain right then was a broken heart. But who, why, and how would anyone want to hear about what I was going through? I was lost. I kept that word but I didn't know what to do with it. So I kept coming back searching for answers. And the next workshop was the one for me. It was on becoming an author and writing an e-book. Bam! There it was. There were editors, publishers, and authors there providing us with the steps on how to do everything from A to Z. Anyone there was presented with a writers course for free. It was awesome and it was all God. He was speaking to me and shed a light on my gift I could share with His people.

And from there God wouldn't let me loose. Because I was diligent at work I was approved to attend a writing workshop during work hours. I initially signed up for it just to get two free paid days away from my cubicle. Not knowing that it was all God's plan. This is how I was thinking, "I have two Master's Degrees. There is nothing a basic writing class can teach me about anything I don't already know." So I went into it already with a bad attitude but was glad to be away from my desk, but I was clearly wrong. The instructor gave us an assignment of free writing on a topic, personal or fiction. She just wanted to see where we were in order to teach us effectively. I initially didn't want to participate but I remembered that I already had notes typed in my phone. Because I was reserved, whenever my precious spouse and I argued I usually shut down. I didn't want to speak because he didn't listen and I was too busy crying. So my outlet was my memo pad on my phone. I would type out my feelings, things I wished he would do to make things better, things he did that really hurt me, and things I wished I was strong enough to say. Some of these were straight notes, poems, and even songs. I had tons of these notes because we constantly fought. They were labeled with dates and times right in my hand. So I used one of those for my assignment and was done.

I didn't want to share my assignment with the class as my instructor had requested. My notes were too personal and I didn't want the people I worked with to know the pain I was experiencing. Instead I waited until our lunch break, apologized to her for my disobedience and gave her my assignment to read silently. And she immediately looked up at me and told me to please share this with the class when everyone comes back. She said I want to show you how profound these words are, how impactful they can be to others, and how many people will pay for this very thing. After much hesitation I did, and the response from the room was amazing. I was told that if this information was given to them earlier maybe they wouldn't have gotten a divorce.

Some stated that this literature could help them with current problems they were having in their marriage. And some told me that they were blessed and informed on ways to handle their future relationships better. I was blown away and grateful. My instructor requested that I look into creating an e-book and send her a copy when it was done - and I did just that.

Every night for three months I went through my daily routine and put my children to bed with prayers. After they were sound asleep, my previous spouse and I would be in our bedroom watching television. Because we usually weren't speaking to each other, I would be on my computer without even a question from him of what I was doing. So I would sit there just about every day and write a little. I would transfer my notes from my memo pad into paragraphs, chapters, and eventually an entire book. I worked with a publisher that I met at my church seminar, with the formatting, editing, and publishing process. The cover was created by a spirit-filled woman all the way in Kansas who wanted to help me make my dreams come true. And the rest was history. I wrote my first book, *Love on Fire*: *How to Maintain the Passion in Your Relationship* in the fall of 2015. This was an accomplishment I never knew I wanted nor seen coming. All of my tears were turned into a piece of literature that would help people make their relationships better by avoiding my mistakes. No one but God could turn my pain into passion and my passion into profit. No one. And He did.

God didn't stop there. From there I started a couple of small businesses that I was able to operate from home. Which I have now combined into one consulting company. And those were created because I needed to do something that made me happy while I was working through God's assignment. Because I gave Him what He asked for, He gave me something in return. And I've loved having my business now called, Bliss Dream Love Consulting, in which I help even more people achieve their personal and professional needs. These visions weren't my own but they were God's. He gave me my business plan, logo, colors, and expertise in my sleep. Every night after I prayed He would give me bits and pieces of this vision that I didn't know what to do with. It took years for everything to make sense to me, but when it did it was amazing.

And the same experience can happen to you and for you. This is the perfect time for it to occur. Why? Because you too are broken in ways that I was and maybe even worse. You are disappointed, hurt, and left discouraged. You may feel defeated and that this is your worst season of your life. If you do I'm so happy for you! Because that means your blessings are coming right around the corner. I encourage you to look at your life and review the pain that you have experienced and endured. And after careful review of that, pray and ask God to show you how you can turn your pain into passion and your passion into profit. Ask Him to rejuvenate your efforts that you put into your past relationships to now be able to put into yourself. Tell Him you are ready for more and to be completely used by Him. Allow Him to completely take control of your life and watch how He will quickly turn things around. The same God that did it for me can surely do it for you. He is just waiting on you to accept His assignment and follow His lead.

Chapter 8
Ask for Help

Owl

Owls are beautiful birds that are known to exist at night. If an owl appears to you in your dreams, it represents wisdom, insight and virtue. And its natural sounds are a warning to some that danger, deception, or even death is near.

"Plans fail for lack of counsel, but with many advisers they succeed." Proverbs 15:22 NIV

"But if any of you lack wisdom, you should pray to God, who will give it to you; because God gives generously and graciously to all." James 1:5 GNT

Whether ending a long term relationship or a marriage, talking to someone else about it is typical. We reach out to friends, coworkers, and some family depending on what the constraints of the relationship were. Whoever our listening ear maybe, we need them. Their comfort, insight, and encouragement can really help us through a tough time. But what if they can't? What if the people we know the most and feel the safest talking to can't help us like we need them to? What if they simply just don't know the right advice to give or guidance to provide? Do we just keep what we are feeling inside and act as if nothing is wrong? Absolutely not. That will only spill over into the next relationship and hurt you both even more. So what do you do when you need help but no one near you can provide it? Seek it elsewhere!

Professional

Despite what some of society thinks, searching for professional counseling or therapist is not a bad thing. It doesn't mean you are crazy, weak, or helpless. It actually shows how strong you are to know and admit that you may need some help. Professional counselors are trained and experienced with helping you learn how to get through the tough times. That's what they do and most are really good at it. They are especially helpful with aiding you in unveiling things from your past that are now affecting your present life. Past experiences and relationships have a direct effect on decisions you could be making now that hinder your happiness. Knowing, understanding, and managing these things can make a world of difference for you.

Therapists are also unbiased. They don't have a dog in the race so to speak. They don't personally have a tie to you or your previous partner. This will allow them to give you the best advice and suggestions possible and present them to you with a clear heart and head. They won't pick sides or favor one more than the other. They will simply guide, support, and encourage you to get through this unfortunate phase in your life.

Sometime after my father passed away I visited a therapist. I was concerned about my well-being and how I handling his passing. Because I was a true daddy's girl, I expected to fall apart after he left. I cried and thought of him all the time, but it almost seemed like I wasn't realizing that he was truly gone. My therapist, who I saw weekly for about eight weeks, helped me understand what I was experiencing. She explained to me that I wasn't in denial, but rather I was at peace. I understood what happened perfectly but was given strength out of my obedience to fully fulfilling all of my father's last requests, taking care of his every need when he was alive, and being the best daughter that I knew to be. From that I was grieving but had a better grip on it than I considered I would previously. She gave me so many comforting words to live by and that further assisted me with the next phase of my life that I was about to face - divorce.

Although at that time I did not necessarily want to divorce my husband, the pain that my marriage was causing me seeped through me in a way that she picked up immediately. I tried to hide it because that wasn't my intent for coming to see her, but I clearly couldn't. Being a trained professional, she knew the meaning behind my words, expressions, and tears. And once she started asking questions, transparency was all I had to offer. I could no longer mask my pain. And I had someone who was there to guide me through recognizing where the pain began, where it affected me most, and how to get passed it. My therapy sessions were my way of being my true self and not being judged. I was able to live and speak my truths without being scared of hurting anyone. It was my personal time and all about me. And I'm so glad I went each week because every time I left I felt twenty pounds lighter. I wasn't carrying around the same baggage that I had for years. I slowly, each week, shed all of the dead weight that was holding me back from being my true self and experiencing true joy. I was free.

Spiritual

Another great way to get insight on your current situation and emotions is to seek spiritual counseling. I'm not talking about psychics or anything like that. I'm suggesting real spiritual guidance under your pastor or church counseling department. Receiving help with someone who will pray for you, uplift you, and speak life into you is an amazing experience. I met with my pastor before my marriage ended and when my divorce was final. I have the highest of respect for my pastor because I know he is truly a man of God. Everything he does, speaks and visions embodies God in every way. That's why it was important for me to hear what his thoughts and advice were for my situation. And those conversations meant the world to me. He simply solidified the fact that God desires for us to be truly happy and live abundantly in every area of our lives. And however and whatever we needed to do to make that happen was our decision. As long as I allowed God to come in and take total control of my situation, lead me, and cover me through my new journey I would be fine. And I did and God has not failed me yet!

If you don't have a relationship with a pastor or specific church that's okay. This would be a good time to search for one. The more you seek spiritual guidance and ultimately get closer to God, the better every area of your life will become. He is literally the answer to every problem you may be experiencing. And the Bible has a story and scripture for every problem as well. I didn't know all the Bible spoke about and how it was so relevant to everything in my life until I started searching. It is filled with guidance from how to come out of debt, how to handle difficult people in your life, and how to learn to love again. When I say everything, it has everything. His word says seek and you shall find. I encourage you to do so!

Group Counseling

Group counseling or coaching is a great way to get help! Whether it is spiritual or not, you will be surrounded by people who are literally walking in your shoes at the same time as you. You will be surrounded by multiple experts on how to get through life's many trials and tribulations in one place. How great is that? It can be really great for you but only if you are comfortable sharing your heart in front of other people. Yes, these groups are typically private and everyone is supposed to maintain integrity for the group by guaranteeing confidentiality. But that's the logistics of it all. The mechanics that makes the group function to the potential it needs in order to help everyone is honesty. You have to be willing to be open and honest with everyone involved. This way you can receive the guidance, feedback, and support that you need.

I experienced a form of this through attending Divorce Care. A friend of mine recommended it after my divorce was final. She had been through it and knew that it could only benefit my new life the way it did hers - and it did. Divorce Care was a thirteen-week group counseling session that guided us through emotions, situations, and possible experiences that we could endure while in the process of separating and/or divorce. Initially I thought I wouldn't like it and that it would be a little cheesy. But it was life changing for me. Every week I gained insight on either something I thought I had handled, should handle, or didn't handle. I learned where I felt the most vulnerable and how to regain the strength my divorce had taken from me. I even learned how there were some things that I did wrong and how to apologize for that as well. Every lesson was wrapped in written scriptures, real life examples, and prayers from the instructors.

The entire experience helped me tremendously through one of the hardest seasons of my life. It showed me how to be made whole through God in order to be truly happy in life whether single or married. I've made lasting friendships with some of my classmates because common hurts and triumphs remarkably bonds people. I was encouraged to share my experiences some weeks and supported if I didn't want to other weeks. It was just a great adventure which makes me confident in suggesting something like that near you if needed. Sharing and learning from others who actually know what you are talking about is one of the greatest feelings ever. Try it out!

Regardless of how you seek help, my advice is simply to seek it. Don't live in a stuck place in your life because you are shamed of what you are and have been going through. That's not what God wants for us at all. We were destined to live great lives by learning from our tribulations. He doesn't want our tribulations to destroy us or stop our growth. So if you need to talk to someone professionally or spiritually to help you get past the pain and learn how to start living again, then do it. And do it now! Life is too short. You only have one, so make it a great one!

> Don't live in a stuck place in your life because you are shamed of what you are and have been going through.

Chapter 9
Moving On with Kids

Sparrow

A sparrow represents rebirth. In faith, the bird stands for the concern of God for the least of all people. These people are always under God's safe keeping. Sparrows are also symbol of peaceful families who live humble and simple lives according to God's will.

"See that you don't despise any of these little ones. Their angels in heaven, I tell you, are always in the presence of my Father in heaven." Matthew 18: 10-11 GNT

"Children are a gift from the Lord; they are a real blessing." Psalm 127:3 GNT

Ending a relationship in general is hard due to all the feelings and emotions that come along with it. It's hard to say goodbye to something or someone you thought would be there forever. Especially when the emotional connection to that person is gone but not the physical due to having children with them. Severing ties with the father of your children is not quite that simple. This is because no matter how they personally have made you feel it has nothing at all to do with the children you share. This is where you put the needs of your child before your own. During this time is when your hurt feelings still matter, but has no bearing on maintaining a healthy co-parent relationship for the sake of your children. Children should never fall victim or suffer because you have a failed relationship. Their minds, hearts, and souls are innocent and should be protected as such. Children should never be punished for what you or their father did to each other.

Explanation to children.

Children are a lot smarter than you think they are at their various ages. They understand, feel, and observe everything. This is especially true regarding their parent's relationships. They understand that one day dad is living with us and the next day he isn't. They feel it when you cry more and don't interact with them the same because of your broken heart. And they observe that their lifestyles and experiences have changed due to a change in income, residence, and family expenses. Your children know. They are human. And they are a part of you. So they have a natural instinct to feel that your natural maternal rhythm is off. As a result of this acknowledgement don't avoid talking to them about the situation. They deserve the right to know what's going on and what is about to happen now that things have changed between you and their father. Trust me transparency and sincerity is the best way to go in this situation. Let me explain further.

Discuss topic with your ex first!

When my pervious spouse and I decided that we would separate physically, we worried heavily about how our children would react to it. They were so young being only five and two years of age. We didn't know how to tell them or what to say. We didn't know what their reactions would be or how it would affect each of us afterwards. All we knew is that it had to be done and time was of the essence.

We had a conversation with each other first before talking to the children. We wanted to be on the same page with our deliverance and language. We agreed for us both to be present and speak so that our children knew no matter what we were still a family. We decided to keep the explanation of what was going to be our new found reality as simple as possible. *We gave examples.* We told scenarios of the not so good times in our home when we argued, yelled, and cried often. We asked them did they understand that this wasn't a good thing and that we wanted to protect them more from seeing that kind of thing. And once my son (because he was older) acknowledged that he understood, we then felt it was alright to proceed. *We gave our solution to the problem.* This was when we went into telling them that in order to protect them from those experiences again we needed to live in two separate places. Mommy would have one house and daddy would have another. (This is when the tears started falling.) My son was so confused at first, but we both were there to help him through this.

When my son really grasped the idea of what was happening he was crushed. You could see it in his face and disposition. He cried and that broke our hearts. We knew that would happen but we had to get through it. *This is when we gave our plan.* We told our son everything. We explained where each of us would live. How and when the visits would happen. How although we weren't in the same space all the time that we still loved each other and would remain a family. We gave him everything. And once he processed this step, *we gave him affirmation.* We reenacted to him that our family meant the world to us both and we are only doing what we thought would make us all happy. We gave him and my daughter hugs, kisses, and high-fives. We wanted them to feel our love, genuine concerns, and sincerity during this difficult time. Essentially, *we gave them both love*.

Although some people would think this was too much for a six year old, we have since learned it was just enough. We see even to this day our talking things out to our children on their level has made this new reality a better one than we could have imagined. My children are not depressed, they don't act out negatively, and they are not angry. They are thriving and enjoying both of their parents in a much happier lifestyle. They are doing great in school and exemplify peace with our new lives daily. This is all due to prayer, open communication, and honesty. We still answer questions they may have for us today and try to remain on the same page with our responses. We work together and still operate as a family. Especially since we are a much healthier one now. So don't be afraid to talk to your children about the next steps. It's their lives, too, and they have the right to know what's happening with it.

Communication with the ex.

Having effective communication with your ex when there are children involved is very critical. It will determine your child's emotional impact during this new experience. Your child needs to witness that you are standing by your word that the family will remain intact, they need to always have access to their dad without any barriers, and they need to see you walk in perfect peace as you continue to not allow your pain to determine progress. There are so many things you have to talk about with your ex when it comes to your children. You all will have to discuss visitation, health care, education choices, financial needs, emotional concerns, and the list goes on and on. It's all about the business of raising your children now. And you can't effectively and successfully do that without some sort of communication.

They are watching!

If it's one thing children will do, it is remembering everything you tell them. They never forget your words, promises, and guarantees on anything. Whether it is that you will take them to the movies, purchase that toy they have been wanting for weeks, or even making their favorite meal. Children don't forget and will hold you to whatever you've promised. And when you don't, their little spirits are shattered. That's because the person who they respect the most has let them down in some way. So best practices are to either, don't mention anything until you can guarantee it to happen or don't say anything at all. Either way, when you do say you are going to do something, try to stick with you.

This shouldn't be any different when you and your previous partner explained to them that despite your relationship failing that you all would remain a family. Those words are powerful and hold so much value in them. It gives your children so much reassurance and comfort to know that this would be happening. It offers them some ideal of consistency and additional support from this already fragile situation - and they will be watching for it. They will be watching how you talk to each other in person and over the phone. They will observe your body language, facial expressions, and emotions when you are holding a conversation.

They want to make sure that indeed everything is alright. And if there are any signs that things are not it can cause a panic in them. This panic can develop into fear, anxiety, and stress if it remains through their observation of a negative situation. And no one wants a child to experience such a feeling like this. Especially from a situation that is not their fault. Although I understand that some situations can't be avoided if a relationship is extremely volatile. But in those cases an effective communication plan can still be in place through a third party. It's all determined by you and the example you want to make for your child. So please if possible, make the best efforts possible you can when you are in their presence.

Not your man, but their dad!

I am a true daddy's girl. My entire life and how I view the world was shaped early by my father. He was my everything. He showed me what real love was, how to show it, and how to express it. I could not imagine not having him in my life. And neither should your child. And a sure way to help prevent that from happening is to learn how to keep the lines of communication open with your ex. This may be hard to do. Especially if issues between you two are unresolved and the hurt is so profound. But it's in the best interest of your child to try. You never want to be the bitter barrier that is causing distance between your child and their father. Your feelings at this time have to be handled at another time. Right now it's about them.

It's not going to be easy at all. Seeing an ex in person, hearing their voice over the phone, or even reading their name in a text message can cause irritation and frustration when your heart is broken. I know because I've been there. I wanted to pretend my previous spouse didn't exist when I was initially going through our separation. One of our biggest problems was communication so I didn't know how I was going to handle this topic. But one thing I did know was that I didn't have a choice. No matter how bad he may have been to me, he treated my children like gold. So they didn't deserve to suffer and experience my pain through my disdain for their father. I had to learn how to communicate with him to make sure they were always taken care of. And the best care they could receive was from the both of us working together.

It didn't happen overnight for us. Sometimes we still argue like wild cats and dogs. That's because we loved hard and the problems that existed within our marriage was never resolved. But the one thing we did learn to do was recognize we weren't talking to each other right, accepted responsibility for our involvement, and apologized. I've received and given more apologies after our divorce than I did during our marriage. And it was from separation, growth and knowing that it no longer mattered how we felt about each other. The only thing that mattered now was those little people that we both created and their happiness. That fact alone was the driver of change for our better understanding of proper communication. Allow it to do the same for you.

Peace & growth through co-parenting.

Effective communication is the foundation for successful co-parenting. It allows both parties to be present, respected, and acknowledge in lives of your children. Which will only foster and cultivate your children to live happy, successful, and prosperous adult lives. This process will not only benefit your children but will also benefit you as well. It is going to usher you into a place of peace and growth from learning how to put your children above yourself. Learning how to humble yourself and work diligently with someone you possibly don't care for is character building. It strengthens you through your pain, hurt, and disappointment. It's making you, not only a better mother, but a better person. Your

> *Effective communication is the foundation for successful co-parenting.*

thought process will be different. Your perspective on parenting will change. And your respect for your ex will possibly increase if they work cooperatively alongside you for the betterment of your children.

Sacrificing your own feelings of disappointment in order to collaborate with your child's father is commendable and will be rewarded. Not that you should do it to be rewarded, but you will be. Initially it won't seem or feel that way. But overtime you will begin to notice how your children will adjust smoothly to their new lifestyle. You will begin to notice that all of those fears you had about your child's reactions will subside. You will see that your child does still laugh when they see their father and are excited for their visits. Life will begin to settle down and become a new normal for all of you. This happened simply because you cared enough to try and gave enough to make it happen. Just watch and see. You will thank me later!

Dating again.

Once you have been made whole and been healed from all of your past hurts, dating may be an option for you right now. It can be exciting and frightening at the same time. But it's a reality you have to face if you don't want to be alone for the duration of the rest of your life. The only thing that's different this time around is that you now are not just dating for yourself, but you have to consider your child as well. This is a package deal that you have to offer, and you must consider that when selecting the next man you may share your life with.

I have been with my same man since becoming a mother. And I clearly remember my dating life before them. So thinking of what that looks like now causes me an uneasiness. I have to consider things I didn't think of before. Like making sure they are not pedophiles, abusive, or anti-children all together. Do they have children of their own? If so, how is their relationship so I can have an idea of how he would engage with mine. Can he handle the noise of children playing early in the morning on a Saturday when he wants to sleep? Does he want to even spend time with just me or with us as a whole? These are just a few of the many questions that run through my head when I consider dating. It almost made me not even want to venture there. I would rather just be alone then chance my children being involved in an unhealthy situation. But then I remembered how old I was and how young my children were, which would make me very lonely for a long time. So I did the only thing I could do, and that was pray and ask God for help.

Take it slow.

When I was feeling all nervous about dating the first thing I remember God telling me was to slow down. I was getting ahead of myself. I was allowing fear and doubt to create negative scenarios in my head that didn't even happen. I ended my future relationships before I even started them - and that wasn't healthy. It was understandable to be apprehensive because my children would be affected by my dating decisions. But it wasn't okay to be so negative about starting a new chapter in my life. One that could lead to true love and happiness. So I had to change my thinking and walk carefully through the process.

The last time I went on a date was a little over ten years ago. The dating world was a little different than it is now. I didn't know what I wanted or the type of man I was expecting. All I knew is that I wanted it to not look or feel like what I've already experienced. I tried talking to a few people and even went out on a few dates. But nothing felt right. I felt like I was only saying yes because I was asked and not because I was interested. I knew that there was no connection or attraction, but I went just for the sake of getting out of the house. And that was a mistake. I wasted time, energy, and money settling because I didn't want to be alone. Each time I heard God tell me that I was moving too fast but I did it anyway. Only later realizing that He was right.

I did it my way before in the past. I let my heart lead me into relationships that my head knew I shouldn't have been in. And look where that took me. This time, I've decided to turn my entire life over to God and let Him take control. This includes my dating life. I want Him to tell me if someone is right or not. I want the green light from Him and only Him. The only way that would happen would be for me to slow down and allow Him to work. My focus no longer became on dating and instead more on Him. As I am increasing my prayer life and strengthening my intimate relationship with Him, His desires for me will be clearer. There will be less of me involved and more of Him. This will be the plan from here on out. I'm enjoying the journey learning God on a higher level. He is showing me exactly what I need, deserve, and will have one day in a husband. And it's something worth waiting patiently for.

Chapter 10
Daddy Lessons- Know Your Worth

Nightingale

The nightingale bird is seen as a symbol of education and excellent teaching skills because it teaches its child to sing beautiful songs. It is also known as a symbol of love and talent.

"But you are a chosen people, a royal priesthood, a holy nation, God's special possession, that you may declare the praises of him who called you out of darkness into his wonderful light. Once you were not a people, but now you are the people of God; once you had not received mercy, but now you have received mercy." 1 Peter 2:9-10 NIV

"Then God said, "Let us make mankind in our image, in our likeness, so that they may rule over the fish in the sea and

the birds in the sky, over the livestock and all the wild animals and over all the creatures that move along the ground." Genesis 1:26 NIV

As I stated earlier, I had the great pleasure of having an amazing father in my life. My dad was the absolute best man I've ever met. He was not perfect, but he was perfect to me. He always made me smile, provided for every need I had, and tried his best to give me whatever I wanted. Other than buying me my favorite toys, cakes, and cars, my dad taught me very valuable lessons about life and relationships. Some things he told me through casual conversations and some things he showed me through his daily actions. Observing him with my mother, siblings, and children I've learned things that can be applied to every relationship anyone can have. His basic principles were all keys to a woman knowing her worth and demanding that everyone treats her according to the rules of her worth. This was especially true with men. He made sure we didn't just allow men to treat us anyway. He valued his daughters as priceless and wanted everyone else to do the same.

This is the same way that God feels about His daughters. We are more precious than gold to Him. My father worshiped and honored God every day of his life. He learned how to take care of us by knowing God. He knew the Bible and tried his best to follow its clear instructions on love and respect. Although as a human, he may have fallen short a few times, he seemed to always get it right when it came to his children, especially his daughters. So whether or not you have a father like mine here on earth, know that you do have one even greater in Heaven. He is the best one to show you how important you are and that you deserve only the best that life and love has to offer.

My father spoke life into us through very illustrative situations and bold statements. He had catch phrases and memorable sayings that we will hold on to forever. Although as young children we couldn't understand the purpose of our father's words and why he insisted on repeating them over and over again. When we became adults everything became clear as day. It made sense to us finally and we recognized, as always, our father was right. Here are a few things that stand out to me while I'm in this new journey of my life. These are some of his favorite principles that helped me through my dating life in the past that I'm positive are still relevant today.

Daddy Lessons!

Lesson 1: A Man Who Don't Work, Don't Eat (Provider)

I have heard this statement my entire life and never knew its significance until I was a young adult. If there is one thing my father was more than anything else was an amazing provider. He had nine children and countless grandchildren, but worked his tail off making sure we were all taken care of.

> _He needs to love you enough to want to do whatever is needed to make your family whole._

My father was a police officer when he went to heaven, but before then he held several jobs in order to provide for his family. Nothing was beneath him. Whatever brought food on our table and put clothes on all of our backs, he did it. He was a pizza delivery man, security guard, and more. He did what he had to do to take care of his family. A man who don't work, don't eat was a phrase for saying in order to get something you had to get up and work for it. The next one needs to provide for you mentally, emotionally, physically, and financially. Although we can't expect men today to be the sole provider anymore, we can expect for him to provide for his family in any way he can.

Provider doesn't mean just financially, but spiritually, mentally, emotionally, and physically. He needs to love you enough to want to do whatever is needed to make your family whole.

Although my father was the sole financial provider of our family, my mother's contribution was just as great. She sacrificed her own personal career to stay home and care for her entire family. She was there to transport us to school, was home when we returned, and there to nurse us back to health when we were sick. And she managed to do all of this with having breakfast and dinner never late, my dad's uniform always cleaned and pressed, house always clean, and got herself together every single day. Superwoman!! But that was her part. Her and my dad had an agreement and they stuck to it with perfection. And that's exactly what the relationships today should look like. An agreement made between two people that exemplify the commitment, but it starts with your provider. If he leads in excellence, you must follow in the same manner.

Lesson 2: Birds of a feather flock together. (Relationships)

My father would often use this phrase when my sisters and I were hanging with the wrong crowd growing up. He would always tell us that no matter who you are, you will always be judged by the crowd of people you hang with. If all of your friends were on drugs, even if you weren't, everyone would assume you were too. No one would just single you out or consider your individual character. So he always wanted us to be careful who we spent and invested time with. He wanted us to be with people who were like minded or better, who were encouraging, loving, and positive. He wanted us to be with successful people in every area of our lives.

My father didn't just talk the talk, but he walked the walk. When he met my mother and started getting serious about our family, he changed his surroundings. Although he was from the streets, he didn't let that hold him there. When he stopped drinking, he didn't hang with those he used to drink with anymore. Rather they were friend or family. He put his own individual family first. He went to church every Sunday, mingled with fellow officers from work, and always spent his extra time with his children. He smothered us with time, even when we thought we were too cool to hang with him. He became the man he wanted to be and only had people around him who supported that way of life.

In essence, my father showed me that a man is only as strong as his surroundings. If your man hangs with cheaters, smokers, drinkers, and liars, more than likely that's who he really is or will soon become. So watch the man you are dating along with his selection of friends and some family. They will tell a lot about his real character. And if he finds himself in these not so positive environments and understands that is not what you are looking for, he will make the necessary adjustments to change it. He has to be willing to support not only you, but the life you two are building together. If he chooses his friends over you, he is definitely not the one.

Lesson 3: A man should always walk on the outside. (Protector)

I remember walking down the street with my dad as a little girl. We were just going to the store to buy some snacks. (My dad loved snacks. It was his love language!) I would always grab his hand and try to keep up with his fast pace. One day I grabbed his left hand and he quickly shifted me over to the right side. He told me that I needed to be on the inside of the street. That I should never walk on the outside near the street when I'm walking with a man. This way if something happens like a car jumping the curb or someone starts fighting, he would be my shield of protection. He said if anyone was to get hurt it was going to be him. As a child I didn't think much of it. My dad was already my protector in every way so I never thought anything less. But as an adult I started thinking about how profound that one was of thinking was for me. My dad was teaching me that any man who truly loves me will always be there to protect me. He will always stand as my shield against anything this world has to offer. He would keep me safe without hesitation. And if he didn't, he wasn't the man for me.

Lesson 4: Don't ever let a man blow his horn at you, that's a prostitute's call. (Respect)

My older sister started dating before me of course. She and I are six years apart. I remember one summer day her boyfriend was coming to visit her. My dad and I were on the front porch. When her boyfriend pulled up in front of our house he blew his horn for her to come out. My sister came outside and began walking towards his car. My father had a complete fit. Although he didn't seem to have a problem with the guy she was dating at the time, he did not like this particular situation. He told me sister not to walk to that car. He said that men blow their horns at hoes and prostitutes to get their attention. They don't have enough respect to get out of the car so the women bend over and talk to them from the street. They are giving their price and getting observed to see if it's worth the package being offered.

This was a scenario he never wanted his daughters to be a part of. So he told her to never do that again. Never respond to a man blowing their horn at you. If he respects you enough, he will park his car, walk to the door, and greet you properly. This gave my sister an attitude because she felt embarrassed, but because she respected him she never did it again. Well at least never while she was still living under his roof! And with me seeing and hearing my dad say this to my sister, I never forgot it. I never did it either, simply out of respect for my father and for myself. My dad was teaching us that a man will only respect you if you respect yourself. Simple message with a powerful impact.

Lesson 5: A man will only do what you allow him to do. (Expectation)

Sitting on the front porch in the summer times with my siblings and parents is a tradition for us. It's a favorite activity that we love to do together. We would talk to each other, laugh with each other, and even share ice cream all together. We were just spending quality time together on our family porch. We still do this 'til this day even in our adulthood. But one summer my father and I were having this conversation about relationships. It started because I asked him why do men cheat on good women. I wanted to know from the one man I respected most why men risk it all for nothing. And he responded by saying men will always try and push the envelope to see how far they can go with a woman. They will see if they can pull one over on you and how you respond to it. If you keep letting him get away with a pass with no consequence, he will do whatever to you because you don't expect him to do better.

My dad said that men will only do to you what you expect and what you allow. What that meant to me is that if I don't have a standard or expectation for myself and the man I'm with, anything goes. In order for either of us to achieve great levels in our relationship we both have to want it, know it, and expect it. Without it we have nothing. And if I allow myself to be continuously hurt by cheaters for the sake of having a relationship, my expectations are extremely low. So I have to raise my standards and not desire more but know that it's what I deserve.

Lesson 6: I smile every time I see you coming. (Love)

My dad and I have always been close. I would stay up at night when I was a child until he came through the door from work. I would listen to his police stories and ask questions to prolong from going to sleep. I followed my dad everywhere he went even more than his very own shadow. But it's during his last two years on this earth that our bond grew even tighter. I came around even more than before and tried to tend to his every need. One day I used my key to come into my parent's front door and my dad was sitting on the couch. This is where he was stationed most of the time due to his illness. When I opened the door and walked in my dad had the biggest smile on his face. He told me that every time he sees me coming he smiles. It made him happy just to be in my presence. He thought me being around him was a gift, not knowing that I felt the same way.

That day stands out to me because if I never felt loved before, I felt it at its highest that day. My dad made me feel so special just because I was me. And being me was enough to make him happy. He didn't judge me. He didn't try to change me. He loved me just the way I was. It was unconditional and forever. It was real, genuine, and sweet. His love for me taught me that my future husband must love me in the same way. It will never compare to my father's love, but it must come close. It must be pure, sincere, and forever. He must cherish my presence and be filled with joy from it. He will value me as priceless and understand my true worth. He has to love me the way God loved his church. Like my father loved me. Without prejudice, stipulations, or requirements. His love will be simple. It will make him smile every time I come in the room.

Lesson 7: I don't care who you believe in, but you better believe in something. (Faith)

If my father was not at work on Sunday mornings, he was at church. He said his prayers every night and whenever he left out to the car in the mornings. He read his Bible occasionally and knew scriptures like they were recipes to his favorite foods. He would shoot one at you in the middle of an argument just to prove his point or position. He loved God and trusted Him with his entire life. This was my example growing up of how a faith based person should live. But my father didn't force religion down us. He never even told us that we had to believe in God. He told me one day that he didn't care what I believed in as long as I believed in something. His only rule was that we honored God while living in his house, but once we were out on our own we had to make our own choices.

Thanks be to God we all remained with his principles. But at least he gave us the freedom to go another direction if we wanted to. He was teaching us that we had to have faith in something in order to survive this world. And that by being the man of our family, he shaped what that looked like for us.

He was the spiritual leader in our home. He showed us how to pray, when to pray, and exemplified life when prayers manifested. He lived by the faith he believed in and tried his best not to be hypocritical. He was the head of our household in every way. He was confident in his decision making and tried to make the best ones for our family. He was faithful in his role and so should the next man I marry be as well. It takes a strong man to lead his family. And an even stronger one to lead by the will of God. That's the one we want!

Lesson: 8: Not everyone gets it right the first time! (Forgiveness)

My dad and I were having a conversation one day on the porch again about relationships. This time he was talking about his first marriage. He told me that his intentions were never to get a divorce. That was something he never wanted because he believed in marriage. But circumstances in that marriage had become so uncomfortable that it was the best for them both. From that he learned that everyone doesn't get things right the first time. Sometimes you have to know when it's not working, let it go, forgive yourself and the other person, and try again. If it wasn't for him believing that, he wouldn't have met my lovely mother and I wouldn't be here.

He was able to learn to forgive himself for failing at something and being strong enough to try again.

Although I was withholding my own marital problems at this time from my dad, the manner in which this conversation happened had me to think my father was speaking to me indirectly. And I heard him loud and clear. I learned that I had to know when a relationship or marriage wasn't healthy anymore and move on from it. No matter how much I wanted it. If it wasn't bringing me joy maybe I wasn't doing it right. And to own my participation in it, forgive myself and move on.

Lesson 9: If don't nobody else got your back, I do. (Trust)

My father made it very clear on several occasions that he was always there for us. Even if we got in trouble and had to hear his raging rant, he was there to get us out of it at the end of the day. He would travel far just to pick us up, bring food to our homes if needed, and even make sure we had money in our pockets to take care of ourselves. Whatever it was we needed, daddy was there to provide it. He used to tell us that he had our backs even when nobody else did. And he was absolutely right. He never let us down. That gave my sisters and I trust. Trust that the one who claimed he loved us really did prove it time after time. Trust that we were never alone in this world. Trust that real love does still exist within family. Trust that we were always taken care of. Trust that whatever he said he would follow through on. Trust that we would never fall because our foundation was strong. Any man that we spend our lives with has to be trustworthy in every area of our relationship. Without it, there is nothing.

Lesson 10: Honor thy mother and thy father. (Accountability)

Out of all the sayings my dad had, this one had to be the most frequently used. My father literally probably said this every day. Honor thy mother and thy father. As children, we used to think it was a scare tactic used to control us and make us follow his rules. It was a little bit of both, but mostly he was instilling something in us. He was teaching us respect and accountability. What we did and said everywhere reflected our parents. We were walking clones of their teachings and lessons. We were extensions of them no matter where we were and should make decisions as such. We learned to honor the rules of our authority figures and live by their standards.

The next man chosen needs to be held to these same standards and be held accountable to God. God is his mother and father that he must honor. He must obey Him in order to be the man that you need and want. He can't feel as if he is his own man and in control of his own life. He can't make decisions for you and your family alone. He must live by God's principles in order to know where to go, what to do, and how to act. Without accountability, he will be unstable in all of his ways. He won't put his family first if he's thinking otherwise. It will be all about him and what he wants. This is not a good quality that you want in a man. You don't want to be led by someone that doesn't have a map on where to go. He has to know that God is his compass, GPS, and pilot. He is the one and only way.

Closing Remarks

Well there you have it! You literally have my heart written out for you. You know my pain, my tears, and how my wing was broken. You have spelled out to you how I experienced one of the hardest seasons of my life and the way God brought me through it. My intentions were not to entertain you but to help guide you through a similar process. God didn't allow my heart to be broken in order for me to stay down. He allowed me to experience such devastating pain so that I could learn from it through my healing. And boy did I ever. Everything I've learned was meant to help others, either avoid going through the same experience or help those who are there now, find their way to peace.

Having a broken wing makes life difficult to go through but it's not impossible. If put in the right hands and fostered with care, it can heal itself. A healed wing will make flight different than before. You won't go the same direction anymore. You will begin a new flight style and pattern that will help you reach your destination more safely next time. It will guide you around winds that could make your journey difficult and through a much smoother path. Regardless of how your new way of flying will be, it will be better. You just have to allow the right hands, His hands, to heal you and prepare you for take-off.

> *But first you have to pick up the broken pieces and place them in God's hand.*

My prayer is that you have learned enough in this book to start making your way toward healing. I know right now it doesn't seem possible but trust me I'm on the other side of it now. It's so much better. You just have to really be ready for it and except all it is has to offer. Be willing to make changes and better decisions in order to protect yourself. As soon as you want healing it will come to you. But first you have to pick up the broken pieces and place them in God's hand. He is the only one that has all of the tools to, not only restore your wing, but make it better.

I am excited for your new journey! I pray it leads you directly toward peace, strength, power, and most importantly love. Love for yourself first, love for your journey, and love for others. You just have to be ready for it. You can do it. I believe in you and I believe in what He can do in your life. I'm a first line witness to it. This won't be easy but I promise it's worth the effort! All you will need to do is be willing and open for God to come in. Allowing Him to make a home in your heart will lead you to a better place. Your life will be in a better position. Your senses will be heightened, your faith with will be strengthened, and your heart will be restored. If you are ready for all of this to happen, I encourage you now to put down this book and go before God immediately. Make one simple requests. Simply ask Him to begin the process of healing your broken wing!

Now it's time to do your work through journaling and prayer! If you're serious about getting through this heartbreak get the *Heal My Broken Heart: Prayers for the Broken Hearted 30-Day Prayer Journal*!

It is sure to be life changing for you as you yield to the process and let prayer and meditation heal you.